Battles with Seminaries:
Defending Israel

*"For Zion's sake
I will not keep silent..."
Isaiah 62:1*

Zola Levitt with Tom McCall

ISBN: 1-930749-39-2

Printed in the United States of America

Dedicated to Israel and her people.

I will bless them that bless thee,
and curse them that curseth thee.
Genesis 12:3

Contents

Part Three: Battle Over Dispensationalism

Introduction

Believe me, I never intended to have a battle with any seminary. In this world, there are enough theological battles to wage with those who are really terribly wrong.

There are the ordinary anti-Semites who, no matter where they attend church or however many Jewish friends they may have, will always look down somehow on the Chosen People. At the Judgment Seat of Christ in Heaven, where all Christians are to appear before the King of the Jews, there will be some embarrassing moments for these people.

And then there are those who say they love the Jews but can't approve of the policies or behavior of Israel. They say, "Dr. Goldberg and lawyer Feinberg are okay in my book, and they are upstanding members of our community. But, oh those Israelis!" Well, I thought about this long and hard, wondering if there really is a way to like some people but oppose their homeland. Can we really ever say, "I like the French but I can't stand France"? I think not. I think those who disapprove of what (the media says) is going on in Israel do so out of that deep-seated aversion to the Jewish people themselves.

Born out of anti-semitism is its ugly daughter, Replacement Theology, the sort of Christianity that asserts the Church has replaced Israel. On that very unbiblical rock, the entire Roman Catholic Church was founded and much of denominational Protestantism. These are people who give real voice to the idea that the Jews are hated by God because they have always been disobedient, even up to rejecting the Messiah.

And the third very large group one should do battle with, if there were time and opportunity, is the liberal Protestants. The idea there would be to somehow get them to open their Bibles and at least become conversant with the nature of the Messiah, the plan of salvation, the coming of the Kingdom, etc. In the majority of American churches, these things are widely misunderstood, and it becomes a serious question as to whether members of liberal denominations will ultimately be counted among Christians at all. If the evangelical idea of each person coming to Christ for his own salvation is true to Scripture, then those who haven't done this just don't have Christ and are not real Christians. But, as I say, these particular strangers to Scripture are too numerous.

So I have not fought real battles against these sorts of opponents. But I have inadvertently stumbled into genuine battles with evangelical seminaries. They are worth telling about, and they are the subjects of this book.

We'll consider just three cases that came to our attention in the past several years in our ministry—a national television program and an outreach offering teaching materials in the form of books, tapes, videos, music cassettes, Israel tours, and the like.

The first case occurred when I chanced to hear a Christian talk show in which a Dallas Theological Seminary professor was insulting Israel. To say I was shocked at his Arabist comments is an understatement! He obviously had become familiar with the propaganda of the Palestinian people. When he finally said,

Introduction

"Perhaps these people [the Jews] might be driven off the land," I'd had enough. I resolved to contact the radio station, its owner, the First Baptist Church of Dallas and Dallas Theological Seminary about what I'd heard. The results of that particular battle will follow in Part One.

After that, I was rather stunned to see a textbook with an awful agenda in use at The Criswell College in Dallas. This is a Baptist school named for Dr. W.A. Criswell, the venerable pastor emeritus of the First Baptist Church of Dallas. The college's former president was Dr. Paige Patterson, a recent president of the Southern Baptist Convention. I would have expected nothing but the most orthodox of evangelical teaching from such a school, but my son brought home a textbook that was totally unacceptable, particularly in the Jewish area. That amazing battle is reflected in the ensuing chapters of Part Two.

And finally, the Lord unmistakably called our attention to an awful doctrine called *Progressive Dispensationalism* being taught at some of the most august and respected seminaries in America. Moody Bible Institute, Dallas Theological Seminary, Talbot Seminary, Biola College, and a number of others teach this error, which is as plain as a mistake in an eighth-grade Sunday school paper.

It's not the theological point that worries me, but the discovery that students coming out of these seminaries and those that teach this doctrine no longer learn accurate End Times prophecy. They present modern Israel and God's wondrous works there in distorted, "politically correct" terms. These seminary graduates, destined to lead churches, will presumably minimize the teaching of the Rapture of the Church, the Tribulation Period, and other relevant eschatology (the study of prophecy and future events), if they teach it at all. As to Israel, they will barely mention the place, convinced that God is not moving there and that the current flood of Jews returning to the land is not a fulfillment of prophecy (although the voluminous prophecy of the restoration of the Jews to the Promised Land is one of the central pillars of Scripture).

Rather than narrate these battles, we have collected our ministry's newsletter articles, transcripts, and correspondence with the principal players such as seminary leaders Charles Swindoll, John Walvoord, Joseph Stowell, and others, and organized them for you to see the real issues involved in struggling with these seminaries. We also have books and tapes based on each battle at our ministry. Ordering information appears at the end of the book.

The most discouraging part of this entire series of battles with seminaries was that I really never intended to contend with anyone. But, in each situation, our ministry was received coldly, if at all, and in the end, was practically cursed for bringing up the point. Rather than receiving letters that said, "Thank you, dear brother, for your sensitivity to things about Israel and the Jews. You do a useful service in correcting our course, and we appreciate it," I received letters practically threatening me and my ministry, and accusing us of virtually setting fire to grand old institutions that were innocent and blameless.

Well, some of our "grand old" evangelical seminaries have gone liberal, as such institutions tend to do over time. The moment to interrupt this awful process is at the beginning, nipping it in the bud. Our seminaries have fallen into nearly secular hands, in some cases, or at least Christians who care more for money and enrollment figures and buildings and banks than for Christ and Him crucified. But the seminaries do not belong to the new administrators and the young professors who teach these errors.

Introduction

They belong to all Christendom. They were established with the gifts of the larger Christian community, and ought to treat those gifts with proper respect. I certainly hope something can be done along those lines.

And I hope it's not too late, "for Zion's sake."

Part One

Battle over the Airwaves

"For Zion's sake, I will not keep silent."
(Isaiah 62:1)

Chapter 1
Firing the First Shot

Christianity Today is a magazine that does not particularly favor Israel as a fulfillment of prophecy or a place where God is moving. I have many times been discouraged by their attitude toward the Holy Land and their editorial policies. In one issue, the magazine was responding to what is often called "Lindseyism," a way of characterizing how God is bringing His people back to Israel and portraying Israel today as a fulfillment of prophecy. I personally favor Hal Lindsey's view on this matter; in fact, I don't think it is even debatable. If one reads the prophecies of the restoration, say Deuteronomy 30:1-5 or Ezekiel 37:1-16, there is no doubt that what we are seeing in Israel today is a fulfillment of those forecasts. Those who disagree either believe there is no such prophecy, or they have relied upon some bogus prior fulfillment of prophecy and have thrown out all future prophecy regarding Israel. I believe that the events we have seen in Israel over the past 50 years verify the teaching of Scripture on the matter.

In March 1992, *Christianity Today* published an article by

Battles with Seminaries: Defending Israel

Ken Sidey, to which I had many objections. It followed the standard "Israel doesn't count" line. I replied with the following fax to the managing editor, David Neff:

> Your cover article in the March issue presented one side of a most controversial matter. Editorial integrity would not permit so lopsided a presentation in a periodical as respected as yours.
>
> Israel is my ministry, my daily work and my first love. My national television programs, more than one dozen books, the songs I compose and my speaking engagements are constantly devoted to the subject of the Holy Land and its present troubles. The prophetic significance of the restoration of the Jewish people to Israel is surely one of the most important Christian issues of this generation, and all sorts of believers take all sorts of views of that phenomenon.
>
> I would like to have equal space in an upcoming issue to present an opposing view thoroughly grounded in Scripture and representing an important sector of the Church and of your readership.

I received no response whatever to this fax or to several others submitted through the years to *Christianity Today*.

The following month, I chanced to listen to a shocking radio interview on KCBI, a Christian radio station in Dallas sponsored by The Criswell College and founded by the First Baptist Church of Dallas. This interview, hosted by Kerby Anderson of Probe Ministries, began with Ken Sidey, the author of the article mentioned above, followed by Dr. Homer Heater, then Professor of Old Testament studies at Dallas Theological Seminary. Not many years before, I myself had hosted a talk show, *Zola Levitt Live*, on this same station and what I heard this day was especially disheartening.

We have pulled together below from lengthy transcripts the key statements of the three men who spoke on this hour-long interview.

Kerby Anderson
Commentator, talk show host
Probe Ministries

In his introductory statements, Kerby Anderson set the tone for this live call-in interview program airing to the Christian community. Dealing often with political issues, Mr. Anderson's show offered up a "controversial area," as he admitted, that of U.S. foreign policy toward Israel. By way of background, Anderson mentions that he has interviewed others about the topic of Israel, including journalists from UPI and *Time*, as well as a Palestinian Christian tour guide. The opening question of the show was: "How should Christians think about the nation of Israel?" So, where was the Jewish-Christian on the show? There are, indeed, many Jewish believers available (I happen to live in the same city) to give the audience a balanced biblical perspective from the Jewish point of view. As you will discover in the succeeding chapters, there was much resistance to our addressing the issue publicly.

Into his discussion with Ken Sidey, his former editor, Anderson indicates dissatisfaction with the mere "theological" argument for the support of Israel.

In the past, certainly the high visibility of people like Ed Macateer and Jerry Falwell have always articulated that "our reason for supporting Israel is that we believe," as it says in this particular ad, "in the Biblical prophetic vision of the ingathering of exiles to Israel, a miracle we now see fulfilled."

But this particular argument is made more in a theological way rather than a political way.

Again, despite the fact that the show was supposed to focus on the *Christian's* view of foreign policy toward Israel, Mr. Anderson indicates here that theological understanding is not enough; political thinking makes one's views more complete. How odd! I would think that we as Christians ought to gather our most fundamental perspectives from the Bible rather than supplant biblical points of view with politics. And the most fundamental perspective on this issue—the nation of Israel in their own land—is that they own it, more than any other nation owns their own land, because God promised it to them and them alone. Israel has a "divine deed" to that strip of land! This basic "theological" fact ought to form the foundation of Israel's dealing with foreigners living within their borders, as well as a Christian's support of the Chosen People.

Yet Anderson believes, as did his guests, that Israel is just another nation and must be dealt with as such:

The minute I raise a question about the Likud Party or raise a question about the reaction of Israel to Palestinians, I usually find myself in a very difficult situation, yet I think if we are really honest with ourselves, both our foreign policy

Firing the First Shot

and even our theology needs to recognize that just because we are to honor Israel does not mean that we then give carte blanche to Israelis for all their political actions.

He states that "our theology needs to recognize" reality, which is, in effect, a relative sort of theological base. My theology ought not to change because of governments and foreign policy and media-driven hype about a controversy. Theology is to be firmly rooted in the Scriptures, regardless of what I believe politically. It cannot change because of current events.

At the end of the hour, Mr. Anderson's irritation is revealed when he says, "I get tired of all the letters. Any letters, send them to Dallas Theological Seminary!" However, after an hour with his guest from the seminary, it was clear that biblical answers to those letters would be hard to find at Dallas Theological Seminary. Rather, the seminary, broadening its theology to accommodate views like Dr. Homer Heater's, would be less likely to respond to questions about God's work in Israel. Since this program aired, further theological shifts have taken place in this seminary and others, movements that minimalize the significance of Israel in the land today.

✡ ✡ ✡ ✡ ✡ ✡ ✡

Ken Sidey
Editor, *Christianity Today*

Although Mr. Sidey is undoubtedly an accomplished journalist, his attempt to present the issue of support for Israel falls short of fairness in his statements concerning the Chosen People and their land. The political situation at the time (e.g., the U.S. loan guarantees) apparently prompted Sidey to survey just how much support there was in the "Christian" community for Israel. He claims, on the one hand, "There continues to be very strong support for Israel across the evangelicals, the Christian conservative spectrum. But especially among, for example, the *Christianity Today* readership," thus equating CT's readership with "conservative" evangelicals.

He also states, "Most conservative evangelical Christians have very strong support for the nation of Israel. And much of that comes from one end of the theological perspective, especially from some of those who would hold to dispensational theology that looks toward a literal fulfillment of many of the Old Testament promises: the restoration of land to the nation of Israel." Furthermore, Sidey specifies that these same supportive Christians "who offer their support see … the modern state of Israel, founded in 1948 as the literal fulfillment, and therefore believe that we, as Christians, need to bless the descendants of Abraham, and thereby be blessed by God." On the other hand, Sidey counters his previous statements by saying that support for Israel, according to his survey, was no longer "automatic," and, in fact, was "declining."

I was intrigued by Mr. Sidey's comment that "Christians tend to *react* [emphasis mine] first of all biblically and theologically, and then look for the outgrowth of foreign policy from that." I'm reminded of the hymn that goes, "May the mind of Christ my Savior, live in me from day to day." The Bible is quite clear that our attitudes toward our world are to be first and foremost influenced and tempered by "the mind of Christ." Philippians 2:5 instructs us to "have this attitude…which was also in Christ Jesus." Galatians 2:20 reminds us that "it is not I who live, but Christ lives in me." Yes, indeed, I ought to "react" from a biblical attitude when I consider foreign policy. Rather than disparage or minimalize those who do, Sidey should be encouraging listeners to look more deeply into their Bibles for answers concerning the times in which they live, particularly in regard to God's Chosen People.

When citing examples from his survey results, Sidey points out that Christians are more and more questioning Israel's "treatment of Palestinians." What about the destructive ways in which the Palestinians treat Israelis? Does Israel send suicide bombers to murder Palestinian families? Does the constitution of Israel call for the annihilation of the Palestinian people? From a historical and biblical viewpoint, who, in fact, are the squatters on the land? Who are the real aggressors? This is Israel's land, given to them by God as an *everlasting possession* and they are defending themselves within their own borders. Why are journalists like Sidey so intent on avoiding the mention of the egregious terrorist activities of Yassar Arafat and his "people," the Palestinians?

Sadly, Ken Sidey seems most gratified with his article about Israel because of the fact that he took no stand whatsoever on either side of the debate. "Really, my purpose was to lay out some of the different players and some of the different positions, not to come down on any one side or the other. So I take some satisfaction that I think I've accomplished that." I'm wondering at what point a person like Mr. Sidey allows the Bible to take him off the fence in order to stand for the Chosen People of God.

Battles with Seminaries: Defending Israel

Dr. Homer Heater
Professor of Old Testament
Dallas Theological Seminary

On the one hand, Dr. Heater states emphatically that he is a "strong friend of Israel" and "very pro-Israel," yet refers to the land as "Palestine," as if this name is synonymous with the nation Israel. Dr. Heater's slip of the tongue in referring to the land of Israel as "Palestine" illustrates one of our major arguments with seminaries and Bible colleges. Rather than insist on biblical terminology for the Promised Land, professors and pastors like Dr. Heater are rather inclined to give little thought to the way in which the God sees His own people, Israel. A professor of Old Testament, above all others, ought to be correcting students and audiences to whom he speaks to emphasize that Gentile believers must be biblically accurate when discussing God's people.

It is clear from this point on in the program that Dr. Heater does not see God working at present in the nation of Israel. It is simply a modern nation, in his opinion, which ought to just cooperate like every other modern nation and put the past aside for the sake of getting along with the Arab squatters on the land. He states:

> I think we need to deal with present realities, and I think both groups—both the Israelis and the Palestinians—tend to go back and pull together historical data to support their cause. And I think we need to deal with present reality, and the present realities are that the United Nations divided the land in 1948, and after the war of 1948 the Arabs had the part that belonged to Jordan and the Israelis had the rest of

it, and we're struggling over that situation right now. I would rather deal with that than try to go back and deal with the past.

How is it that this professor of Old Testament language and history—*Jewish* language and history—can actually say that the Chosen People of the Old Testament should just forget about their own history? Ought the people of God just give up their "divine deed" to certain parts of the land promised through the Abrahamic covenant—an unchangeable covenant—and accept the man-made decision of the United Nations?

Heater emphasizes the future hope for Israel, but concludes that today the Jews in Israel are no different from the Arabs and must get along with them like any other nation.

He believes that peace is likely, that there is "an unprecedented opportunity for peace." Again, however, he sees Israel as the one who is preventing peace, claiming that the Israeli "settlements on the West Bank are one of the greatest obstacles to that peace." He is quick to speak out, as so many in the media do today, against Israel's so-called, "provocation of the Palestinians." Could anything be more pro-Palestinian, anti-Israel than statements like these? Where is the outrage over the Palestinian attempts to destroy Israel? Even a caller had to remind the "experts" at the interview that "the Arab leadership doesn't want to dispossess Israel. They want the Jews dead."

Dr. Heater makes one of his most forceful statements of the program when he suggests that God will perhaps drive Israel out of their land. He is so intent on not seeing God at work in Israel today that he must put blinders on, as it were, when it comes to prophecies related to Israel. What happened, may I ask, to the soon coming Rapture of Jesus, a doctrine which

Battles with Seminaries: Defending Israel

Dallas Seminary has traditionally held? Read what he says:

> [The Jews in Israel are] not the fulfillment of prophecy.
> And I think that's where we will disagree with a lot of people,
> because most of the people who have called in have argued
> that what's going on is a fulfillment of prophecy, and there-
> fore we can't touch it—it has to be left alone. And I per-
> sonally would disagree with that position. I think it's pos-
> sible that God ... even conceivable that Israel could be driven
> out of the land of Israel, and still be brought back in that
> eschatological sense that the prophets speak of it. And so,
> I'm reluctant to see all of these things that are happening
> today directly tied in with prophecy.

How tragic to not see God at work among His Chosen
People in their own land! As a final statement on the issue, Dr.
Heater again attacks only the Jews for holding up a real peace:
"They have to be held accountable to do the things that are just
and equitable."

Incidents like this radio interview continue to sadden me
deeply because at the heart of these statements is a profound
disrespect for God's Chosen People, and, indeed, for God's
plan itself. Yes, there will be a great spiritual awakening among
the entire nation of Israel in the future Tribulation period and
Israel will be saved. Yes, there will be a *complete* fulfillment of
the restoration of the Jews to their land during the millennial
reign of Christ. But how can anyone, particularly Old Testament Christian scholars, fail to see that God is presently pre-
paring His people for those future events? How can one deny
the miracle—yes, miracle—of God bringing the multitudes of
Jews from around the world back into their own land, the Prom-

ised Land? It is happening, right before our eyes, and it's time that the Christian community, especially those who teach pastors-to-be in our seminaries, go back to their Bibles and to their theology and see that God is indeed at work among His people today!

Chapter 2
The Heart of the Battle

Variant Biblical attitudes regarding the nation Israel, such as those propounded by Ken Sidey and Homer Heater, point to the very heart of the battle in which we've been engaged for nearly a decade. Did God just abandon Israel during the first century or will He bring them back into the land promised to Abraham, Isaac, and Jacob? Is the state of Israel today a fulfillment of God's prophetic working or is it merely a work of man, not to be regarded by the Church as significant? What attitude ought believers today have toward Israel?

Dr. Thomas S. McCall, our ministry's Senior Theologian, responded to this disturbing radio interview with the following letter to Kerby Anderson, setting forth with superb biblical clarity the proper Christian attitude toward that small, but vital, nation to which we will shortly be going to reside for 1,000 years.

Thank you for sending me your "Israel Packet," which I have read with interest and growing concern, along with a copy of the tape which I received of your recent radio talk show on KCBI with Ken Sidey and Dr. Homer Heater. I do not believe we have met, but I am a fellow graduate of Dallas Theological Seminary, served in Dallas and Los Angeles for some 25 years as a missionary for Christ among the Jewish people, and have co-authored several books with my friend and colleague, Zola Levitt.

If I understand your position correctly, you and your colleagues are premillennial with regard to the Second Coming of our Lord, hold to the pre-Tribulation Rapture, believe in the future blessing of Israel and in the unconditional nature of the Abrahamic Covenant. In all of this we are certainly in agreement.

However, you also seem to believe that the modern state of Israel has no relationship to the fulfillment of Biblical prophecy. On the contrary, you feel that this episode in Israel's history may well be a transitory human effort, and that the Jewish people could, and probably will be, "driven out" of the Land again until such time as Israel receives the Lord Jesus Christ as Messiah. Only then will the Jewish people be allowed to dwell in the Land. The reason, you say, the Jewish people have no Biblical right to posses the Land at this time is because they are in a state of disobedience to God by having rejected Christ Jesus.

Therefore, because in your view the modern state of Israel is not Biblically prophetic, Christian believers in the Bible should not consider the Jews to have any special claims upon the Land at this time, and the counter claims of the Arabs and Palestinians should be given equal, if not greater, weight than the claims of the Jews. I believe this is a fair statement of your position; please correct me if it is not.

Permit me to share with you my convictions, as you

seem genuinely interested in having an informed debate on this matter. I believe that the modern state of Israel is indeed the beginning of the fulfillment of Biblical prophecy with regard to the restoration of the Jewish people to the Land, the Northern Invasion of Israel, the Tribulation, the rise of the Antichrist, the Abomination of Desolation, Armageddon and the Second Coming of Christ.

The Scriptures make it clear that Israel will *initially* be returned to the Land *in unbelief.* This would appear to be the significance of the "Dry Bones" vision in Ezekiel 37. The dry bones are seen to be gathered together out of the graveyards of the nations, but have no life in them. Subsequently, God breathes into them and they become vibrant with life. Our conviction is that this refers to a gradual process in which the Jewish people return to the Land in unbelief, but by the end of the Tribulation they are ready, willing and able to receive Christ at His return. This is the view reflected in many Christian publications and films, including the classic film on the subject, *His Land*, produced by the Billy Graham ministry.

Indeed, it seems that the Jews *must* return to the Land in unbelief in order for many of the prophecies related to the Tribulation and the Second Coming to be fulfilled:

1. Sign the treaty with the Antichrist (Daniel 9:25).
2. Rebuild the Temple by the middle of the Tribulation (Daniel 9:24-27; II Thess. 2:4; Matt. 24:15).
3. Mock the Two Witnesses of the Lord in Jerusalem (Rev. 11:7-11).
4. Receive Christ in Jerusalem at the *end* of the Tribulation, when He returns to the Mount of Olives (Zech. 14:4).

Furthermore, to indicate that God would allow Israel to become a nation again after two millennia of dispersion, remove them and then bring them back to the Land yet again for the Second Coming, would be to charge the Lord with playing some kind of cruel game with the Jewish people. Such a scenario is purely speculative, with no Scriptural warrant.

It is therefore my conviction, along with many other evangelical believers, that the modern state of Israel is part and parcel of the divine prophetic plan to return the Jewish people in unbelief to the Land in the End Times, and prepare them for the difficult events of the Tribulation, and the glory of the Second Coming of our Lord.

What, then, should be the position of the Church corporately and individual believers in Christ with regard to Israel in such a time of prophetic fulfillment?

First, we must recognize the fact of the Jewish *ownership* of the Land by reason of divine decree in the unconditional Abrahamic Covenant. This is a unique situation, and one that must not be taken lightly by anyone who believes the Bible. No other nation on earth has a written divine land grant of a particular section of the planet. Only Israel has such a land grant. Gentiles cannot rightfully claim ownership of this Land, nor can the descendants of Abraham through Ishmael. The only people who have a title from the Almighty to this Land are the descendants of Abraham through Isaac and Jacob. Thus no Christians, Gentiles, Arabs or the United Nations have any rightful say as to the *ownership* of this unique Land. That is a matter settled forever by God. We must keep this fact concerning rightful ownership in mind in any discussions about the Land. Ownership has much bearing on any considerations concerning legal rights.

Possession of the Land is a different matter. God has allowed Israel to possess and be dispossessed of the Land several times during the 4,000 years since the Abrahamic Covenant was enunciated. However, God never allowed man to decide whether or when Israel would possess the Land or not. He always made the decision, and never delegated that decision-making power to anyone else. The Jewish people possessed their Land during times of both obedience and disobedience to the Lord in the Patriarchal period, the Judges era, the time of the monarchy, in the days of the Second Temple, and in the Church Age. Who besides God has the authority to decide whether the Jews should or should not possess the Land to which God has given them everlasting title? Should we Christians arrogate that authority to ourselves? Should the Arabs? Should the Gentiles? Should the United Nations? How dare we or anyone else take it upon ourselves to decide whether it is all right for Israel to possess the Land which they own by unique divine decree?

Inasmuch, therefore, as I am a Gentile believer in Christ and His inerrant Word, I recognize the right of Israel as the perpetual owner of the Land, and the right of God to allow the Jewish people to repossess the Land whenever He chooses. As a believer in the Prophetic Word, I further recognize that Israel must return to the Land in unbelief in preparation for the Tribulation and the Millennium. I am constrained then to realize that the current development of the state of Israel in my lifetime is the beginning of the fulfillment of these prophecies. I cannot accept the alternative notion that the Lord is playing some kind of cruel cat-and-mouse game with Israel, in which the current possession of the Land is a hoax and is of a transitory nature.

If, therefore, we believe that the current state of Israel is of God, and is the beginning of prophetic fulfillment, what should our position as Christian believers be concerning the enemies of Israel, most prominently the Arab nations and the Palestinians who would destroy Israel if they could, and drive the Jewish people there into the Mediterranean Sea?

I believe we should urge the Arabs and Palestinians to welcome Israel as the best thing that ever happened in the Middle East. I believe that if they welcomed Israel with open arms, God would bless them beyond all measure. Already, with their very grudging non-tolerance of Israel in our time, God has blessed the Arabs with the discovery of the greatest oil reserves and wealth in the world. What have they got to complain about? It boggles the mind to imagine what would happen if the Arabs would say to the Jews, "This is your Land, God has given it to you forever. Come, occupy it, and we will do whatever we can to help facilitate the immigration of Jews from around the world. There is room and enough wealth and enough in the Middle East to share and to spare!" Surely the windows of Heaven would open in blessing if they would take such an attitude.

Alas, after over forty years of cold and hot wars in the Middle East, built upon 4,000 years of mutual distrust between the descendants of Isaac and Ishmael, such a welcome is extremely remote, and it is almost laughable to propose such a policy. Nevertheless, I cannot help but think this would be the will of God for all parties concerned. But what if this is not done? What if the animosity and acrimony continue, as appears highly likely? What position should

Christian believers take?

I believe we should support whatever policies would enable the Jewish people to possess their own Land. What of the Arabs, the Palestinians who have lived in this area for generations? My observations lead me to believe that they desire to live there as part of Israel. This would be particularly true of the Arab Christian communities in Nazareth and Bethlehem. They never fared very well under Moslem rule, and they have flourished under Israeli rule, until the PLO moved in and began threatening them for cooperating with the Israeli government.

But many of them, mostly the Moslem Arabs (although some of them would like to remain in Israel), would prefer not to live under Israeli rule. What should our policy be toward them? We could agree with them that they have more right to the Land than the Jews, but this would be a denial of the Biblical land grant and the End Time prophecies, and we must not deny the Word of God. We could urge the surrounding Arab nations to provide refuge for them, but they have been reluctant to do so, primarily because to leave the Moslem Arabs in Israel gives the Arab nations leverage in their struggle against the Jewish nation. What if the United Nations, including the Western Powers, were to offer refuge and voluntary resettlement to the Arabs living in the Land of Israel who wanted to leave? What a revolutionary concept! Many thousands would undoubtedly accept the offer as a desirable solution of a very difficult personal situation. I believe the nations could absorb this influx without too much difficulty if they were willing. Most Arabs would probably prefer to live in a Moslem country. This offer from the nations might actually shame the Arab countries into offering refuge to the Palestinians themselves, which really seems the most logical solution to a very difficult problem. If we are convinced as Bible-believing Christians that the Jews have an inherent Biblical right to possess the land which they own, God willing, then this kind of solution would appear to be the most humane policy we could urge upon the nations. It would be better than war, better than trying to force Israel to give up possession of the land which God has given them, and better than allowing this situation to fester without offering a humane solution.

There are Biblical examples of Gentiles who assisted Israel in its possession of the land. Notable are Rahab and Cyrus. Rahab represents the non-Jewish inhabitants of the land who recognize that God has given the land to the Jews, and they offer to help them even if it meant that their own people would be dispossessed of the Land. Rahab was willing to give up her Canaanite claim on the land because of her faith in the Word of God and His promise to give the land to the Jews. God greatly blessed Rahab, saved her family, and actually made her an ancestress of our Lord Jesus Christ.

Cyrus, on the other hand, represents Gentile governments who recognize the right of the Jewish people to possess the land. Such possession was vehemently opposed by the then-current inhabitants of the land (the Samaritans) and the surrounding countries, and they tried every way to annul the decree by Cyrus that the Jews could return to the land to rebuild their Temple, Jerusalem and their nation. God greatly blessed Cyrus by naming him as "His Anointed" one through the prophet Isaiah (44:28-45:1) over 100 years before his birth, and by granting the Persians a long and prosperous empire.

We now face a similar situation as Rahab and Cyrus faced in the time of the first and second occupations of the land by the Jewish nation. The third occupation has begun, and the Jews are returning to the land, just as the Scriptures indicate, largely in unbelief. It should be noted, however, that there is a sizable minority of Jews in Israel who are believers in Jesus as their Messiah, just as in New Testament times. They are enduring a difficult struggle, but they are having an increasingly strong testimony in Israel. They are precursors of the 144,000 Jewish believers in Christ who will bear witness to the Lord during the Tribulation. We must not ignore the struggling church of Jewish, Arab and Gentile believers in Israel today.

But as to our attitude toward the revived nation of Israel, do we stand with Rahab and Cyrus, or do we side with the multitudinous enemies of Israel? I trust we will strive to serve the Lord and support the possession of the land by Israel.

I would greatly appreciate your thoughts on these arguments and positions. If there is a genuine debate on this matter among evangelical believers, perhaps we can reach a consensus that will move the nations in which we reside to a Biblically correct and humane solution that will honor the God of Abraham, Isaac and Jacob, even the God and Father of our Lord Jesus Christ. Ultimately, of course, we realize that there can be no truly lasting peace until the Prince of Peace returns. Even so, come quickly, Lord Jesus.

There was no response to Dr. McCall's eloquent letter.

In our May 1992 monthly newsletter, I shared with our readers this ongoing battle against anti-Semitism on KCBI. Excerpts of that newsletter follow:

> We are seeing some controversy over modern Israel and its claims to the land, some of it in the most Christian of "Christian circles." Recently I heard Professor Homer Heater of Dallas Theological Seminary on a broadcast hosted by Kerby Anderson of Probe Ministries. Our ministry called and requested that I be included as an additional guest on this program. We were told that the program was going to be "balanced" and "non-confrontational," there was no room for another guest, and that, if I wanted, I could call in to the show.

"Balanced?" I thought at the time. How can a program about Christian attitudes toward Israel and the Middle East be *balanced* without including the perspective of a Jew, particularly a Messianic Jew? I wanted to do a lot more than call in, of course, because Professor Heater made some provocative statements on the radio that truly did require a biblically-balanced response.

> "It is not the fulfillment of prophecy," said the Professor, supposedly learned in the Old Testament, discussing the restoration of the Jews to Israel that we have seen in this generation. I didn't realize that prophecy fulfillments were up to Dr. Heater to judge. In other parts of the program he said that he loves Israel very much, but the people are disobedient. Again, I thought it was up to God and not Dr. Heater to judge who was spiritually obedient in this world.
> To come to the point, I was flabbergasted by the subtle

anti-Semitism I heard on this offensive talk show. The host made the point that, in his opinion, Israel's political positions tend to nullify it as the fulfillment of God's blessings to Abraham. He also gave verbal credibility to the notorious Committee for Open Debate, the obnoxious group which declares that the Holocaust never happened. The conglomeration of soft-spoken theology, Christian do-goodism, garden variety anti-Semitism and neo-Nazism was simply stupefying.

Jew-hating which masquerades as profound theology, "I-Love-Israel-for-Biblical-Reasons" protestations, government policy, "fairness" in listening to various dissident groups, or so-called freedom of expression in journalism, is *still* Jew-hating. It is divinely punishable under Genesis 12:3. Let me quote it again word for word so that everyone, particularly these anti-Semitic commentators, are clear on its meaning: "And I will bless them that bless thee, and curse him that curseth thee." The most dangerous anti-Semitism is spread by those who don't recognize they're anti-Semitic.

This newsletter will chronicle anti-Semitism as it happens, until the day the King of the Jews comes and puts a stop to it. By the way, I have requested to be on Mr. Anderson's radio program in order to present a truly balanced view. I'll let you know how it goes if he has the guts to confront a Jew with his anti-Semitism.

Listening carefully to the personalities on this talk show, I concluded that all three can honest-to-goodness look in a mirror and think they're lovers of Israel, while what they say can lead to another Holocaust. It's become "politically correct" to side with the Palestinians and criticize the Israelis. No doubt the Antichrist will put to good use the philosophies of such polite, well-meaning and downright vicious "authorities."

Chapter 3
First Baptist Church of Dallas

As a member of First Baptist Church of Dallas, the church that founded The Criswell College and its radio station, KCBI (K-Criswell Bible Institute, named for First Baptist's distinguished pastor emeritus, W.A. Criswell), I decided to bring the matter to their attention with the following letter to Dr. Joel Gregory, then pastor of the church. It was my desire to see the church take decisive corrective action upon one of its own institutions.

On April 9, your radio station, KCBI, broadcast a most anti-Semitic program. I was very deeply distressed by it at the time, and it's difficult for me to forget the issue. As a matter of fact, I intend to draw national attention to it.

I devoted this ministry's monthly letter, which is mailed to some 45,000 subscribers, to this issue. A copy of this letter is enclosed. It will apprise you of the details about this program and my feelings about it.

As a member of First Baptist Church, a faculty member

emeritus of Dallas Baptist University and a former KCBI talk show host, I'm going to come forward and tell you I will not tolerate defamation of Israel and the Jewish people: not in government, nor in education, and most certainly not in my church. As the enclosed letter will attest, I have twice previously volunteered to come forward in a more gentle way to try to balance this issue, but was rebuffed both times. I've had enough brushing off now, and I am going to make some specific requests:

1. A meeting with you personally, in which I will explain the doctrinal errors presented on your program. I wish at least to tell you what was said in the name of First Baptist Church. I will be accompanied by Dr. Thomas S. McCall, a long-time member of First Baptist Church and a theological consultant to this ministry; Richard Thomas, the ministry's general counsel; and my son, Mark Levitt, the ministry's operations manager.

2. A public retraction by your talk show host of what was said on this program as regards credence for the so-called Committee for Open Debate, a neo-Nazi organization.

3. An appearance on the program—with or without your host. And this time the people who call in will be honored with a hearing. (Virtually 100 percent of them disagreed with the personalities on the program, but were courteously dismissed.)

I have recently consulted with another, much larger ministry to the Jews. That ministry, too, finds an escalation in what we might call Christian anti-Semitism, a horrible distortion of Biblical doctrine. You would be amazed at the backlash that can come at those who curse Israel.

Rather than express outrage at the anti-Semitic interview hosted on KCBI, Pastor Gregory responded with this disconcerting letter (italics mine):

I am distressed by both the content and the tone of your recent letter. The situation which you mentioned regarding *a comment* by Dr. Homer Heater on a KCBI broadcast *does indeed deserve attention.* However, in your haste to confront this *perceived slander* against Judaism, you have set off down the wrong path.

KCBI radio is neither owned nor operated by First Baptist Church, Dallas. Ownership and oversight for this Christian radio station belongs to the trustees of The Criswell College. Any complaints regarding the operation of that station should be taken up with that Board of Trustees.

I sincerely wish you had checked the accuracy of your information before publishing your remarks in the monthly newsletter of your ministry. Your misrepresentation of the position of First Baptist Church, Dallas, may do irreparable damage to the reputation of our church within the Jewish community. Your very membership within our church body serves as an imprimatur regarding our Christian support for Israel. The hasty publication of inaccurate statements does not reflect well the biblical injunction to deal privately with a brother concerning mutual differences. I urge you to clear up this issue in your next newsletter.

With regard to the meeting which you suggest, I recommend that you pursue contact with the appropriate oversight committee of The Criswell College Board of Trustees. Their next semi-annual meeting is scheduled for Monday, May 18.

I trust you will pursue this matter with a measured fervor. May God bless you *as your actions glorify Him.*

In our newsletter, I printed the following response to Dr. Gregory:

I was deeply hurt by Pastor Gregory's letter. I awoke in the middle of the night, full of conviction about what to do in defense of the Promised Land and my people, and that is what I'm doing. In the above letter an hour of degradation of the Chosen People is reduced to "a comment by Dr. Homer Heater" and a "*perceived* slander against Judaism." The pastor asserts that the situation "does indeed deserve attention," but gives it none whatever.

The second paragraph is an infamous government dodge. "You need to go down the hallway to some other office, sir, and they will process your complaint." I certainly thought the pastor of this enormous church might be concerned about what is broadcast on a station whose call letters (KCBI) stand for "K-Criswell-Bible-Institute," Dr. W. A. Criswell being the venerable pastor of this church when I joined it. In any case, reporting the felony to the wrong court doesn't excuse the felony.

In the third paragraph, the notion that I have reported to the wrong office is summed up with "misrepresentation of the position of First Baptist Church" and "inaccurate statements." There were, of course, no inaccurate statements in my letter. Other than presenting my own views, we quoted word-for-word from our tape recording of the program.

But the point about my membership in the church was the stunner. I can't determine if the pastor meant that my choice of this church for my own worship reflects that it supports Israel, or whether my being accepted by this church, even though I'm merely a Jew, indicates this church's gracious position toward Israel. The first case is certainly true; when I joined the church under Pastor Criswell, it was most supportive of Israel, and I thought it still was. If the pastor meant the second case, it is an unchristian insult. Christian people, even pastors, do not properly rule on who may come to church. If it came down to that, then it is *he* who is accepted within *my* church if I read the New Testament correctly. In either case, I'm extremely troubled by the implication that I am somehow different from other Christians and that my appearance in a major Christian church is somehow remarkable. The most subtle form of bigotry is to be singled out as a special case among one's peers.

The lecture on my failing "to deal privately with a brother" is simply not factual. As I pointed out in last month's letter, I twice approached the talk show host about an appearance on his program and was twice rebuffed, though I think I would be considered an adequate spokesman on the issue of Israel. No one cared, or cares now, to hear about the pain of a Jewish believer on being publicly excoriated in Christian media.

The pastor invites more public discussion when he urges dealing with the issue further in my next newsletter. That's what I'm doing. I'm sorry that he did not simply take action, but I believe he underestimates the gravity of the charges.

And finally, regarding the pastor's closing remark, "May God bless you as your actions glorify Him," I thought defending Israel *was* a glorifying task. God Himself has never failed to do that, in agreement with His everlasting covenant made with Abraham. Anti-Semitism will be a thing of the past only when the King of the Jews, with His forgiveness for me, for you and for the First Baptist Church of Dallas, rules and reigns here in all His fullness.

I am very sincere and speak from the bottom of my heart when I ask you for your comments and your responses. Believe me, I don't want to use this newsletter, which serves as part of the financial lifeline of this ministry, for this purpose. We are a tiny organization compared with this very powerful church. But this is a task this ministry will never shirk. I am naturally afraid of arguing with huge organizations, but I am even more afraid of anti-Semitism. Six million of my people were slaughtered by those who attempted to cover up the Holocaust. Sadly, their bloody work was sometimes facilitated by misguided churches in the care of misguided pastors.

In response to our exposure of this growing Christian anti-Semitism, many wrote to the various personalities who were attempting to push aside the gravity of these events. The prayers and actions of those who truly love God and His Chosen People, Israel, were indeed effective. In response to our requests, just before the publication of the above article, KCBI agreed to have me on their talk program in order to present a defense of my brethren in Israel and of God's current prophetic work in the Jewish nation today.

Additionally, we were able to meet face to face with Dr. Homer

First Baptist Church of Dallas

Heater and the executives of Dallas Theological Seminary regarding his views on Israel. God opened these doors in order to allow the truth about His people to be defended.

Chapter 4
Dueling with DTS

In May 1992, we were finally invited to meet with the officers of Dallas Theological Seminary, Professor Homer Heater, Kerby Anderson, etc. From our ministry, I brought Dr. Thomas S. McCall and another theological assistant, along with my son, Mark, the Operations Manager of our ministry, and Richard Thomas, a board member. I remember thinking that it was like the Jewish *minyan*, a quorum of ten men who meet for prayer.

The meeting got off to a rocky start. Professor Heater looked me in the eye and said unctuously, "Brother Levitt, I want you to know that I have nothing but love in my heart for Israel." I could not help but reply, "Professor Heater, please love someone else for awhile. With love like yours, we can't get along."

And on we went with my confronting Heater with his anti-Israel positions and his exclaiming, "I never said any such thing," only to be exposed with a transcript of the radio program containing his comments word for word, and this in front of the President and Vice-president of Dallas Seminary.

By the following term, Professor Heater no longer taught

at the seminary, and I was just as glad. I have tolerance for every kind of disagreement except over Israel. And if I'm to be accused of being thin-skinned on that subject, then I'm guilty. However, I think I'm on safe ground with God where Israel is concerned.

After our meeting, Dr. McCall wrote the following letter to Dr. Donald Campbell, then President of Dallas Theological Seminary:

> May I take this opportunity to thank you for moderating the meeting the other day when we met with the seminary professors and leaders of Probe Ministries to discuss evangelical Christian attitudes and theology relating to modern Israel. Enclosed is a copy of my letter to Kerby Anderson reviewing our views on the subject, and I would appreciate any comments or suggestions you may have.
>
> We are grateful for the sound teaching and positions you, Dr. Walvoord and the Seminary have historically had concerning the Jewish people and Israel, and trust it will continue until our Lord's return. It became clear to us in the discussion that there was a significant distinction between your view concerning modern Israel and that of Dr. Heater. For instance, as I understand, you feel that Israel must have the West Bank area in order to protect its natural security against its enemies. Dr. Heater, on the other hand, believes that Israel should not interfere with the Palestinians on the West Bank nor build any Jewish settlements there, because it is unnecessarily "provocative," and is a violation of international law.
>
> All of this may seem like a minor disagreement over geo-political disputes, but at the heart of the matter are our attitude and understanding of the land grant given by God to Israel, and the implementation of the occupation of the land by

the Jewish people in the prophetic End Times. These are Biblical, not just political, issues. It would seem that anyone who believes in Christ and His Word would be very concerned about attempting to erect any roadblocks that would hinder Israel from occupying the land which God has given to them. This is where we fear this new movement among evangelical brethren would lead. At the very core, it seems that they would withhold from Israel what God has promised to Israel, and by so much they are against Israel and against the will and revealed Word of God. We are delighted that you are not among those who would move in that direction.

I know Zola Levitt also appreciates your re-invitation to speak at a chapel service at the seminary, probably next fall, so that he can share with the students his concerns from the Word.

Although I had been assured that I would be given equal time on KCBI to rebut the aberrant views of Ken Sidey and Homer Heater, it was an uphill battle to actually secure a commitment from Probe Ministries as to the time of the interview. It appeared that by stalling, they could simply allow the reaction to Dr. Heater's interview to fade away with forgetfulness. Finally, at the end of June, one day before going to print with our newsletter, I wrote to Jimmy Williams, director of Probe Ministries, demanding he keep his promise to air our side of this crucial matter.

At last, Dr. McCall and I were welcomed at KCBI studios to appear with Kerby Anderson on the talk show. We made a transcript of that program and have issued the tapes from our ministry under the title "The Anti-Israel Tapes." We urge you to obtain a copy.

In the meanwhile, Dr. Campbell answered Dr. McCall's letter. Dr. McCall wrote in response to some of the points he made in his letter.

Thank you for your kind response to my previous communication. I appreciate your taking the time to think through and articulate your convictions. Surely one of the major issues of the day is how believers in Christ relate to the remarkable phenomenon of modern Israel. It certainly has a bearing on our attitude about the Second Coming of Christ. Your own remarkable effort in hosting 19 pilgrimages to Israel is marvelous testimony to the Biblical and prophetic significance of modern Israel to evangelical Christians.

One thing that puzzles me is that you feel that our saying that Israel is the beginning of the fulfillment of Biblical prophecy is an unwarranted dogmatic position. It seems evident to us that modern Israel is the beginning of the restoration of the Jewish people to the land in unbelief, as depicted in the vision of the Dry Bones in Ezekiel 37. The brethren I have discussed the matter with have a similar conviction and cannot understand why we should not believe and teach this conviction. To us, it appears to be perfectly consistent with our premillennial, pre-Tribulation Rapture view.

I would appreciate it if you would share with me why you are reluctant to assert this. Is there some theological problem I am overlooking? Please let me know.

You realize that there are those who not only do not assert that modern Israel is the beginning of the fulfillment of prophecy; on the contrary, they assert that Israel is *not* the fulfillment of prophecy. For instance, when Dr. Heater was on the radio program with Kerby Anderson, there is the following inter-change on the tape and the transcript:

Dr. Heater: It is not the fulfillment of prophecy. And I think that's where we will disagree with a lot of people, because most of the people who have called in have argued that what's going on is a fulfillment of prophecy, and therefore we can't touch it—it has to be left alone. And I personally would dis-agree with that position. I think it's possible that God—not possible, I think God *is* using all this as part of His ultimate plan. But it's even con-ceivable that Israel could be driven out of the land of Israel, and still be brought back in that eschatological sense that the prophets speak of. And so I'm reluctant to see all of these things that are happening today directly tied in with prophecy.

Kerby: I think that's well said. I've said that before, but I'm glad you're saying it. I get tired of all the letters. Any letters, send them to Dallas Theo-logical Seminary!

Since the above program was broadcast on KCBI, Zola and I have had opportunity to confer with Kerby and be with him on this same radio program. I believe he has mod-erated his position considerably. But it is apparent that there are those associated with the Seminary and other evangelical ministries that contend the current state of Israel is not the ful-fillment of prophecy. Our Jewish brethren in Christ feel this is tantamount to separating the modern Jewish people from the Biblical hope of the future of Israel. Thus, it is felt to be a betrayal of Jewish believers and a movement of evangelical Christians away from a belief in the unconditional promises to Israel. This is why we are so concerned about the issue.

At any rate, I think it would be helpful if you would clarify for us why you believe it is unscriptural or theologically unwarranted to assert that modern Israel is indeed the beginning of the fulfillment of prophecy.

In response, Dr. McCall received the following memo from Dr. Campbell's office. It is a digest of End Times prophecy by an unquestioned expert, Dr. John Walvoord, chancellor of Dallas Theological Seminary. Dr. Walvoord takes a middle-of-the-road view on modern Israel, allowing that it is indeed the first step of End Times prophecy.

This will acknowledge receipt of the letter from Dr. Thomas S. McCall which you [Dr. Campbell] have forwarded to me, and also your previous correspondence with him.

It is difficult to state this in a memorandum so that it will not be misunderstood. I will attempt it as requested by your secretary.

I believe both Dr. Heater and Dr. McCall are somewhat inaccurate in what they are saying. When we say prophecy is fulfilled or unfulfilled, we first of all have to state what prophecies we have in mind.

In my frequent interviews on secular radio, I was often asked to explain the significance of current events in the Middle East, and I had to summarize this in a very brief form in order to get it into the radio program. I often would say that my belief is that there are a series of future events, the first of which is the Rapture of the church; this will be followed by the emergence of a ten-nation group in the Mediterranean which will revive the Roman Empire as stated in Daniel 7:7, 24. These ten nations are not named but undoubtedly will include southern Europe. When these ten nations are formed, a dictator will arise who will gain control of three and then later all ten, as stated in Daniel 7:8 and other passages that refer to the ten kingdoms as a unit. From this position of power, he is able to impose a seven-year covenant on Israel of Daniel 9:27, which will bring relative peace to the Middle East. During the first three and one-half years Israel will prosper, but their prosperity will be interrupted by an attack by Russia and other nations to the north described in Ezekiel 38-39. The invaders, however, are destroyed by the supernatural intervention of God, but it serves to exalt the dictator of the ten nations who apparently is the object of attack by these northern nations. From the additional power and prestige given him, the ten-nation leader then makes himself dictator over the whole world at the mid-point of that last seven years. He apparently is accepted by the world as its dictator without a fight; he allies himself with Satan, breaks his covenant with Israel, becomes their persecutor as well as the persecutor of all who will not accept him as God. This introduces what Christ called The Great Tribulation. This three and one-half year period is described in the Book of Revelation from chapters 6-18. According to Christ, it was so awful that if He did not stop it by His Second Coming after three and one-half years, no human beings would be left in the world. This is brought out in the terrible catastrophes in the Book of Revelation which, if taken literally, devastate the world and leave perhaps only ten or twenty percent of its population intact. At the close of the three and one-half years, a world war breaks out with Israel as the battleground. This refers to Armageddon, a geographical location in Northern Israel, but which actually covers the whole area. At the height of this war and even while there is house-to-house fighting in Jerusalem, the Second Coming of Christ occurs according to Zechariah 14:1-3 and Revelation 19:11-15.

These events are interrelated and are cause and effect in that one has to follow the other. The problem of interpretation of prophecy is that the Rapture, which I believe is the first event, is given no signs in the Bible. Accordingly, theoretically it could have happened any time from the first century till now as there are no preceding events outlined.

In surveying this whole field, it is obvious that prophecy falls into three major areas: prophecy relating to the world, prophecy relating to Israel, and prophecy relating to the church. I did not usually include it, but the world church seems to emerge in the first half of the last seven years, and is destroyed by the ten nations at the mid-point in order to make way for the world dictator to be God. Now the question is, is prophecy being fulfilled today? Obviously some prophecies are. Christ said that the church would be built upon the foundation which He laid, and of course, nineteen hundred years have witnessed the rise both of the professing church and of the true church—the body of Christ. In Deuteronomy 28 it makes it clear that Israel was to be scattered all over the world. This has been fulfilled and continues to be fulfilled to the present day. Prophecy indicated that Israel would have a hard time in their dispersion and that many would be killed but that they would retain their individual and national identity, which is a marvelous illustration of the accuracy of prophecy.

In view of all this, what are the events of the last fifty years that would lead a person to believe that the Rapture could be near?

What we are seeing are not signs of the Rapture, but preparations for events that will follow the Rapture. These can be itemized. According to Scripture, one of the first events after the Rapture will be the formation of the ten-nation group. Until recently this was impossible because the nations of Europe have been fighting each other for centuries and never have had peace. In order to have a ten-nation group, the nations have to be in a peaceful relationship to get together. Suddenly after World War II, because of the Common Market, the nations formerly fighting each other became friendly and today the threat of war in Europe has decreased, particularly now that Russia is no longer a factor. This is an amazing new development that has taken place in the last fifty years. The Bible also indicates that in the last three and one-half years before the Second Coming, there will be a world government, but this has to be built upon the acceptance of the people of a world ruler. In our twentieth century for the first time, a real world government has been contemplated, and of course has its preliminary recognition in the United Nations. There has never been anything like this in the entire history of the world.

It is also true that for the first time in history, the mechanical things for a world government are in place, that is, we have rapid transportation, rapid communication, computer control of finances, and missile warfare. All of these things will play in the hands of a world ruler. In fact, without these, a world government would be impossible. In other words, our world situation the last fifty years has changed dramatically until what the Bible predicts for the events after the Rapture could naturally take place.

In regard to Israel, all prophecies at the End Time preceding the Second Coming picture Israel in the land (cf. Matt. 24:25ff). There were not any large numbers in the land before 1948 and they were not recognized as a political state. The fact that Israel is in the land is a precondition for the fulfillment of prophecies that will occur after the Rapture.

Further, as I understand Israel's restoration program, it has four elements. First, the covenant state of Daniel 9:27 when the peace treaty of seven years is imposed. This is followed by three and one-half years of peace. This in turn is followed by three and one-half years of The Great Tribulation—the time of Jacob's trouble—and this will be followed by the Second Coming of Christ. This order cannot be reversed, but the whole program cannot begin until Israel is a political unit. As long as Israel was scattered all over the world, it was impossible to have such a peace treaty. In 1948 this stage was set for such a peace treaty, and to me it constitutes a most important development.

Whether this is called fulfillment of prophecy or signs of the times indicating we are moving into the end time may be debated.

The assertion is made by Professor Heater that Israel could be driven out of the land again. While this is theoretically possible, it does not fit in the pattern of God's dealings with Israel. When they came back from Egypt, they came back as a nation, and even though they failed God in the wilderness and wandered for forty years, they did not go back to Egypt. When they were carried off to Assyria and Babylon, when they came back there in fulfillment of Jeremiah 29:10, only fifty thousand came back but this constituted the return predicted by Jeremiah 29:10. Having four million Jews in Israel is an unprecedented movement of the nation that cannot be ignored.

The Bible also predicts that there will be a final regathering of Israel to the Holy Land at the time of the Second Coming of Christ. Obviously, this has not been fulfilled. But before this can happen and before the Second Coming of Christ can occur, there has to be a preliminary partial regathering of Israel in order to set the stage for end-time events. This is precisely where we are today. Accordingly, whether this is a fulfillment of prophecy or not may be debated, but it certainly is a sign of the times. When Christ was on earth the first time, the religious leaders did not recognize the evidence that He was the Messiah in fulfillment of prophecy. We have the same situation in the world today where the church at large is totally oblivious to the many things that are happening that are in keeping and in preparation for future events in prophetic fulfillment.

Israel's return to the land today is not a fulfillment of their ultimate restoration, but it is the first step which necessarily has to precede the steps that follow.

When you add to this the formation of a world church movement which is also a part of the twentieth-century phenomenon, you have preparation for prophetic fulfillment among the nations (or the Gentiles), among Israel, and among the church. These three major areas all converge on the same idea that the stage is set for future fulfillment. This is what I have been preaching, this is what I contend in my book on *Armageddon*, and I believe we are living in prophetic days.

It follows, however, that we cannot set dates. One of our professors at the Seminary said, "You have been predicting the Lord's coming for a long time, and it hasn't happened. Doesn't it prove you are wrong?" The answer, of course, is no. The Rapture is always imminent, but that doesn't mean that it is necessarily soon. We have some evidence that it may be soon, but this kind of evidence is not sufficient on which to set dates. Accordingly, it may take some time. But I resist the idea that it is going to take centuries before this is fulfilled, and I believe there is evidence that the Lord's coming is near as I have indicated.

I was grateful to Dr. Walvoord for taking the time to respond to this important situation. Eventually, I received an invitation from Dallas Theological Seminary to speak at their student chapel service the following semester. I did that to mixed reviews. It seemed to me that the audience of students had already been conditioned by Dr. Heater's views on Israel. On the other hand, as I left the stage, one of the professors seated behind me on stage actually took my hand and squeezed it meaningfully (albeit out of sight) to indicate his support for what I had to say. I began my talk that day with the remark, "I have come here to remind you not to forget your first love, Israel." Imagine having to stand at an evangelical school pulpit and try to explain to a disbelieving audience that Israel—mentioned on every page of the Bible, and to which the entire church is going for 1,000 years—is important!

The following is a letter to Dr. John Walvoord from Dr. McCall:

Dueling with DTS

Dr. Campbell has forwarded to me your excellent memo relating your views on the restoration of Israel and the Second Coming of Christ. Your clear explanation of these great Biblical events have always been a great joy to me and to multitudes within the body of our Lord.

As you so clearly indicate, most of the prophecies pertaining to Israel relate to the Tribulation era after the Rapture of the church, so we could only expect to see their foreshadowing and not their precise fulfillment during the Church Age. However, there is one prophecy I would like for you to clarify for me, and that is the vision of the Dry Bones in Ezekiel 37.

There is clearly a process involved in the fulfillment of this prophecy:

1. Dispersed Israel comes out of the graves of the Gentile nations.
2. Dispersed Israel comes into the land as "dry bones," for the most part in unbelief.
3. Israel receives Christ, is given the Spirit of God, and is fully established in millennial blessing in the land.

I have always understood that what we are seeing today is the beginning of the fulfillment of this prophecy. The dispersed Jewish people are coming out of the graveyards of the Gentile nations in which they have suffered all these centuries. They are coming into their ancient land and have re-established their nationhood among the family of nations. With about four million Jews already in the land, about one-fourth of the world Jewish population, they appear to be well on their way.

They are, of course, returning for the most part in unbelief in Christ, and therefore are "dry bones," but this is precisely what we would expect in the fulfillment of Ezekiel's vision. It should be noted also that there is a struggling church in Israel today, composed of believing Jews, Arabs and Gentiles throughout the Land, and they are maintaining a witness for the Lord Jesus Christ there.

Could you please share with us what your views are about the vision of the Dry Bones of Ezekiel 37? Is what we are seeing today, the return of some four million Jewish people, the beginning of the fulfillment of this great prophecy? It would be most helpful to us and to many of those who study the Word to have a clear understanding of this prophecy and its fulfillment.

Thank you for your kind assistance in this matter.

We did not get a response to Dr. McCall's letter to Dr. Walvoord.

I must not forget about Dr. Homer Heater, whose remarks began this first "battle" of ours. In February 1993, Dr. Heater sent the following letter to me:

I am writing to say thank you for our conversation Tuesday. I sensed a genuine conciliatory note in your words.

As I think about your suggestion that we get together for non-confrontational discussion (which I agree would be a good idea), I believe it would be helpful if you would print a retraction of your charges against me contained in your newsletters of May 1, 1992, and August 1992. Since you said to me personally, "I do not believe you are anti-Semitic," it would clear the air if you would state that in your newsletter. As you know, things in print take on a life of their own, and I would not be surprised to hear people quoting your original charge for the next twenty years. I have prayed and thought considerably about whether I should ask you to do this or simply accept the situation as something the Lord would have me bear. I have come to the conclusion that I should ask you to do it.

If you will make this good faith gesture, I will then be delighted to sit with you and Tom or anyone else for a constructive conversation.

God's best in your work for Him.

In March 1993, I sent Dr. Heater a timely article from the *Jerusalem Post* and included the following letter:

Thank you for your letter of February 10. I also appreciated the discussion with you at the Seminary, which the Lord evidently arranged providentially, and look forward to getting together with you, so we can discuss together our views about modern Israel in a non-confrontational atmosphere.

With regard to your suggestion, let me assure you that we never stated in our newsletter that you personally are anti-Semitic. What troubled us so profoundly, and still does, was that you were supporting positions and attitudes that appear to us to be anti-Israel, anti-Semitic and, indeed, unscriptural. That is why we feel it is so desirable to meet with you further to discuss these matters.

Perhaps our understanding of your views is inaccurate.

If so, we would like to have a clearer idea of your position. If not, we would like to know the process by which an evangelical, premillennial Christian professor has come to the views which you have espoused.

As you can well understand, this is no minor issue to us. The attitude of the evangelical Church toward Israel in general, and the Jewish-Christian movement in particular, is a high-priority concern in our ministry. We have discovered that the Muslim hierarchy, the Palestinian Arabs, and the Middle East Council of Churches have joined together to persuade Christians to withdraw support for Israel, and are "rewriting" the New Testament to do so. We interviewed the author of this article, as well as Palestinian representatives, who confirmed that all of this was actually happening.

As an Old Testament professor in one of the most highly respected evangelical and premillennial seminaries in the world, you have considerable influence on the thinking of those who will be leaders in the Christian world, especially with regard to the place of Israel in God's plan and the fulfillment of prophecy. For all these reasons, we feel that further informal discussions with you could be mutually beneficial.

Please let me know a time that would be convenient for us to get together.

From *The Jerusalem Post*, Sunday, October 4, 1992:

"The Churches' Anti-Israel Crusade"

Dueling with DTS

It is hardly surprising that Jerusalem's Anglican Bishop Samir Katify has decided to co-sponsor, with a world Islamic organization, a conference on the situation of Christians in this country. The move is consistent with the local churches' growing involvement in the political drive for a Palestinian state.

Indeed, to expect church leaders in Israel and the administered territories to tend to their flocks and stay out of politics may be unrealistic. They are, after all, as vulnerable as lesser mortals to terrorist pressures. But it is a pity that just as the Vatican seems to be abandoning—albeit timidly and slowly—its fierce refusal to recognize Israel, these church leaders are joining in Yasser Arafat's campaign to form a Moslem-Christian front against Israel.

The campaign began a decade or so ago, when the PLO embarked on an attempt to "de-Judaize" Jesus and "Palestinize" him. Palestinian Arab Christians like Hanan Asrawi have made the absurd claim that they can trace their ancestry to the first Christians, even though there were no Arabs in the area until the Moslem conquest in the seventh century. Yasser Arafat has described the apostle Peter as "a Palestinian who defied Rome." And a Jordanian TV production earlier this year blamed the Jews for murdering Jesus, "the Palestinian prophet."

Instead of protesting this ludicrous rewriting of history, some in the Christian Arab clergy—including Latin Patriarch Michel Saba and Riah Assal from Nazareth as well as Kafity and Ateek—appear regularly in the foreign media as PLO propagandists....

Cemeteries have been desecrated by Palestinian Arabs.

Slogans like "Islam will win" and "First the Saturday people then the Sunday People" have been painted on walls, and PLO flags draped over crosses. Two years ago a PLO flag was painted on one of the domes of the Church of the Holy Sepulchre.

In the Bethlehem area, threats and intimidation prevented Christian families from celebrating Easter and Christmas for several years; these celebrations were regarded as a violation of the Intifada. Christian shops which remained open despite Intifada-proclaimed closures were set on fire. Last year a Christian pilgrim, a woman of 64, was murdered near Manger Square. If Christians are leaving the area it is because they feel their existence and their children's future are threatened, not by Israel but by the rise of Islamic fundamentalism.

That the churches have pointed an accusing finger at Israel rather than at the PLO and the Islamic fanatics is another sign of consistency. When dealing with the Arab world the pronouncements of the leading churches are clearly affected more by political considerations than morality. During the Gulf crises, for example, the Pope spoke out 38 times against the war, calling the anti-Saddam Hussein effort "a threat to humanity," and offering his prayers for Iraq.

Monsignor Henry Teissier, president of the North African Conference of Catholic Bishops, said at the time: "We Christians of the Arab nations…rejoiced while listening to the Pope. We found in his words confirmation that there is no identification between Christianity and the Western world."

Dueling with DTS

I realize that reading letters, portions of past articles, and radio program transcripts is a bit difficult in putting a story together. On the other hand, these are the authentic documents we have from this undertaking. I hope that the point was made that an anti-Israel attitude in Christendom is simply not acceptable. Liberal Christians, sacramental Christians, etc.—the un-Biblical "Christian" church—have been anti-Semitic from day one (the first century), but those who read the Scriptures have no excuse for this.

Frankly, Dr. Heater wasn't the first person expressing anti-Jewish sentiment I've run into in the Christian world, though in general evangelical people are kind to the Jews and sympathetic to Israel's situation. But it was my first encounter with the sort of high-minded officials of Christianity who talk down to what they consider to be common parishioners, as if there is some hierarchy in the church.

The true Christian church has no hierarchy. There are only two levels of Christians—One went to His Father 2,000 years and then we have the rest of us, all level at the cross. There are no important Christians. Some are busier than others. The pompous language and terribly unctuous spiritual announcements of those in the "ivory towers" must deeply grieve our plain-spoken Lord who, among all descriptions of Him, "told it like it was."

All in all, I had good feelings about the treatment from Dallas Theological Seminary and First Baptist Church. The seminary was fair enough to grant me a high-level meeting and a chance to speak in the chapel as well as on the radio program. Officials at First Baptist "lower" than the pastor soothed my feelings by telephone and, in the end, the church relented and is more careful about Israel and the Jewish people. They even sponsor a Messianic congregation these days.

Battles with Seminaries: Defending Israel

Professor Heater and I did not have our face-to-face meeting but, while I bear him no malice, I would have told him very forcefully that his positions about Israel were un-Christian. While there's a glimmer of a chance that modern Israel is not tied in with End Times prophecy, I would say that the likelihood is 1% in view of what I read in the Bible. A professor of Old Testament studies ought to have read the same passages.

Anti-Semitism (or anti-Israelism or anti-Jewishism) is a subtle, ongoing sin in the church. It ought not to be among us at all because it is a doctrine from God's enemy. Obviously, if the devil could get rid of the Jewish people, he'd have little problem with the Christians. They would feel that studying the Scriptures—which would be a relic book of an extinct people—was meaningless. Soon everybody would be an unbeliever, and I don't know where God's Plan would go from there.

In the present day, we are battling another form of the same anti-Israelism, the doctrine of Progressive Dispensationalism. This commonplace error is being taught at many Bible schools, and has at its roots a simple aversion to Jewish people and their land. More on that in our upcoming section on Progressive Dispensationalism.

Textbooks are critically important in training graduates of any educational institution, but especially important when training pastors of future churches.

Seminaries, therefore, must take real care in what textbooks they select since their graduates will be influential through the Christian community. If the textbook is somehow in error and the student is nevertheless convinced of its teaching, then that error will be transferred to the next generation and so forth.

Our next section deals with a particularly wrong-headed textbook discovered by my younger son, Aaron, when he attended The Criswell College.

Part Two

Battle over Textbooks

Chapter 5
A Textbook Case

Wise King Solomon said in Proverbs 10:19, "When there are many words, transgression is unavoidable." How true that is for all of us, and particularly true in Christian publishing. Today, Christian writing runs the gamut from romance series to how-to books to doctrinal treatises. Much of it, unfortunately, makes me queasy. Often in my reading I find that Scripture is watered-down or left out completely in a so-called Christian publication. Or, the views on Scripture in many books are simply in contradiction to sound biblical doctrine. This is not to say there are not any good books out there, but my point is that believers must read with biblical discernment because most publishers—Christian publishers—are no longer concerned with sound doctrine as much as they are with bestsellers. In fact, a number of Christian publishers are allied with or have been bought out by secular companies, as many Christian recording companies are. What used to be the nation's largest Christian book distributor is now owned and operated by the largest secular book distributor. What is the result? Unbelievers are many times making decisions regarding the editorial policies and marketing of Christian publications. Thus we must, above all else, be careful when we pick up a "Christian" book. And this is exactly how our second battle began—our battle over textbooks. Here's how I explained it to our readers in our June 1998 *Levitt Letter*:

"Of making many books there is no end," (Ecc. 12:12). That would be fine with me if they were all good books. But sometimes I run into something really discouraging.

One of our ministry's most tedious duties is responding to churches, seminaries and the like to correct their anti-Israel and anti-Jewish biases. When my son, Aaron, went to a Christian high school, a teacher said one day that Christianity did not start in Israel, but actually in Greece. I ended up sitting in the principal's office, having to inform a so-called Bible teacher that thousands of people were saved in Israel at Pentecost, in Antioch, in Ephesus, etc., before the Gospel took real root in Greece. I informed him that Jesus Christ is Jewish. So were all of His disciples and all of His apostles. I explained that all of the New Testament writers were Jews and that Christianity is part and parcel of Judaism. I reminded him that Jesus came to this earth and declared to His disciples, "Go not into the way of the Gentiles, and into any city of the Samaritans enter ye not: But go rather to the lost sheep of the house of Israel" (Matt. 10:5,6).

I was discouraged that this teacher, in a denominational school, had so little comprehension of Scripture. Most of the large denominations put the Bible away long ago and are almost unaware of the roots of their faith.

I was relieved when Aaron graduated and went on to Dallas Baptist University, and then to The Criswell College to take up serious Bible studies. But lately I have been very disappointed. A perfectly awful textbook called *A Survey of the New Testament*, by Robert H. Gundry, is in use at both colleges. It is the most anti-Israel, anti-Semitic and Biblically wrong-headed textbook I personally have ever seen. I used to teach at Dallas Baptist University, and I realized then the sober responsibility of those who would train future pastors and other ministry workers. I would not have had such a book in the same building with my students. Let me give you a few quotations:

Trying to leave out the Jews, the author asserts, "'And they glorified the God of Israel' (Matt. 15:31), shows that the 4,000 whom Jesus now feeds are Gentiles." This preposterous idea on the part of the One who said "I am come only unto the lost sheep of the house of Israel" (Matt. 15:24) is followed by a vain attempt to create a non-Jewish following of Jesus. The author goes on, "Together then, with the preceding Gentile woman and, earlier, the centurion and the Magi, they represent the great mass of Gentiles who are flocking into the church of Matthew's time." Naturally, there was no Church in Matthew's time, nor any "great mass of Gentiles" saved in the Gospels, though they are to come in considerable numbers later on.

The author subscribes to Replacement Theology: "Matthew writes his Gospel for the Church as the new chosen nation which, at least for the time being, has replaced the old Chosen Nation of Israel."

"Luke was probably a Gentile...his name is Greek. His facility in using the Greek language also suggests that he was a Gentile." The same things were true of Paul, certainly a Jew and a "Pharisee of the Pharisees." Other inane arguments on this point are contradicted in an excellent study by Dr. McCall entitled "Was Luke A Gentile?" which appears in the March 1996 issue of the *Levitt Letter*. You can read it on our website at www.levitt.com.

When Peter converts Cornelius, he has to "defend himself against parochially-minded Jewish believers in Jerusalem who criticize his going to the Gentiles." Naturally these Jewish believers were questioning Peter because they had never seen Gentile salvation before. Evidently they missed author Gundry's 4,000 Gentiles fed, followed by "the great mass of Gentiles flocking into the Church of Matthew's time."

I could go on and on. This is a book a competent Bible teacher can open almost anywhere and want to laugh, or cry, out loud. Truly the author has an agenda to promote an anti-Israel Replacement Theology doctrine, and he utterly misunderstands the mission of Jesus Christ, who came, as He said, to bring the Kingdom to Israel. If secular colleges are bothered by PC (political correctness), the Bible colleges need to watch out for PD (Progressive Dispensationalism), the awful doctrine behind these distortions.

This must be the first book on the New Testament whose index does not even mention Israel. The book refers to the land as Palestine, has a map called "Palestine in the Time of Jesus" (as does the new *MacArthur Study Bible*), and calls Peter, John, etc., Jesus' "Palestinian disciples." I can't say it strongly enough: this textbook is a travesty. I am amazed that any believing Christian anywhere would try to defend it.

When Aaron originally came to me, troubled about what he was hearing in class and reading in this textbook, I consulted Dr. Tom McCall, Senior Theologian of our ministry, and asked what to do. Aaron had selected 49 different passages that were unacceptable, even to a 19-year-old freshman Bible student. Dr. McCall, an ordained Baptist minister and theologian of great experience and skill, counseled me to schedule a meeting with the college administration. We discussed the fact that these two colleges were not unique. Dr. McCall mentioned other conservative seminaries, including Moody Bible College and Dallas Theological Seminary, whose doctrines concerning Israel seem to be subject to Progressive Dispensationalism. I would appeal to our readers and viewers to ask questions at their own local Bible schools about such doctrines as amillennialism, Progressive Dispensationalism, and all the other fancy "isms" for cutting Israel and the Jews out of faith in the Jewish Messiah. The problem seems endemic. Of course, the liberal seminaries, the public media, and certain Christian magazines are a lost cause on this issue. They have long ago written off the family of our Lord.

But back to The Criswell College. Aaron and I met with the President and the Executive Vice President, and we discussed his 49 points. We were treated courteously and both administrators substantially agreed with all of our complaints. They seemed disappointed and taken aback that such a textbook had gotten into their college. They knew the author's doctrine was suspect, they admitted. They told me they would correct the situation in good time. Two months later I was obliged to write and ask if anything was being done. And nearly six months later I finally received a letter *defending the textbook*—even defending the use of the term Palestine for the Israel of Jesus' time!

This is a good place to insert the letters we received from The

Criswell College regarding their response to our concerns about Gundry's book. It is important to note the progression of their comments as the months passed.

After Aaron and I met with Dr. Lamar Cooper in early December 1997, Dr. Cooper sent us a letter that announces the fact that this matter is important to him and will be addressed.

"I wanted you to know that Dr. Wells [Criswell's president] and I take very seriously what you had to share with us. I further appreciate all the material you left for me to review." Then he proceeds to tell us how busy he is and how he plans to speak to the faculty about the textbook on January 14, 1998. Further, he states, "I have had one brief conference with Dr. Wolfe in which I have conveyed to him that based on my knowledge of Robert Gundry alone, the Gundry text is not one that I would have selected." Dr. Cooper sounds sincere. He's been made aware of a bad book. He already knows the author of that book, Gundry, is not of great character—"based on my knowledge of Robert Gundry alone"—and he would not have chosen the book had he been teaching the course. This sounds good. It sounds responsible. He's knows it's a problem. He's going to deal with it. He says, "I have reserved specific comments or observations until after I have reviewed the text myself." Dr. Cooper concludes his letter in the following manner:

Thanks for your patience in allowing us time to work through these details. You have brought us an important point which I recognize needs to be addressed with our faculty. The selection of textbooks needs to be a matter of utmost care considering the fact that freshmen will be extremely impressionable and most of them come to us as a blank slate. They have not had the background or training to view controversial textbooks with discernment. Thanks for taking time out of your busy schedule to give us your input.

I felt like The Criswell College would do something about this matter. They were grateful to us for bringing the subject up. They express that it was "an important point." They acknowledge that freshman students are "extremely impressionable," unable to "view controversial textbooks with discernment." These strong statements about the school's concern over the matter put me somewhat at ease. Out of courtesy, I was patient. However, as you will see, my patience was taken for granted. In retrospect, this first response from Dr. Cooper threw us off.

January came and went, and I did not hear how the school had decided to deal with the textbook. I wrote to Dr. Cooper again on February 4, 1998 to find out the school's course of action on the matter. On the 10th of that month, I received another reply from Dr. Cooper, but this time, the importance of correcting the textbook problem had begun to wane.

Dr. Cooper first explains that he had, in fact, not reviewed the textbook as announced in his December letter. He also states that the Gundry text was not in use for the spring semester. I suppose he felt more at ease because of this point and perhaps surmised I would just drop the matter. "I consider this matter to be *too important* to rush to judgment…I want to be able to give a well-documented response to you, the faculty, or any others that might want to know why we are dropping the text, *if that is what we decide to do.*" [Emphasis mine] Wait a minute! I thought he said that he knew all about Robert Gundry and would not use his textbooks. Now, he's not so certain he would drop the text from the curriculum of the school. This is where, I believe, the breakdown in the attitude of The Criswell College towards the text begins. Dr. Cooper concludes this letter by stating, "While I have begun to look at the material, I cannot give you a fixed date when I will finish." Now it was obvious. He did not take it "seriously" in December in order to address the faculty on January 14 as announced. He feels that since the book was not up for use in the spring semester, it's a non-issue for now. Finally, he tells me not to expect a response anytime soon. If the use of the book is "too important to rush to judgment," then it's too important to set aside until the next incident of its use in the classroom. If indeed Dr. Cooper was too busy to review the text in a timely manner, then he could have had a faculty committee look into the errors of the text and review their conclusions with him.

Nearly six months passed since Aaron and I first brought this matter to the attention of The Criswell College and still no word from Dr. Cooper about the book. Finally, on May 1, 1998, he sent me the following letter, again begun with excuses for his delay [on such an "important" matter!]:

I am very sorry to have taken so long in fulfilling my pledge to get back to you regarding our conference in December and the issues presented in writing relative to Robert Gundry's book. I have been finished with my review of the material for more than a month but have not been able to sit down for the protracted time needed to give the kind of reply needed. I began typing this response on April 7 and it has taken these several weeks to complete the document and get it ready to mail.

This was not a good start in my opinion. The "document" which had taken several weeks to complete was just over two pages long! In it, Dr. Cooper addresses ten or eleven points about our concerns regarding Gundry's anti-Israel stance in the textbook. Below are just a few highlighted for you:

- All of our faculty members are premillennial and all are dispensational to some degree. Not all would be dispensational in the more classical sense of, say, Schofield [Scofield] or Walvoord.
- Whether Gundry is the best text or not (I happen to think it isn't), our professors are free to choose their textbooks. We will continue to do this unless someone were to choose a text which contained statements contradictory to our published statement of faith. So far as I can tell, Gundry's text does not contradict our statement of faith.
- I have read Gundry's statement on page 187 in which he says he believes the 4,000 mentioned were Gentiles. He further sates that these "represent" or are symbolic of the great throng of Gentiles who came to trust in Jesus as Savior in the time of Matthew.
- "Replacement theology." Note that Gundry says on page 161 that the church "for the time being" has replaced Israel, which indicates it is not a permanent replacement. I can't find any statement that indicates Gundry believes the church permanently replaced Israel.

First, Dr. Cooper admits that the school is not as dispensational as entering freshmen (or their parents) are led to believe. Although there have been debates about C. I. Scofield's expressions of dispensational theology, Dr. John Walvoord's defense of the dispensational doctrines have been normative for decades, at least until the recent onset of "progressive" dispensationalism (which we cover in Part Three of this book).

Dr. Cooper also states that the Gundry text is not out of line with the doctrinal beliefs of the college. I suppose this implies that, doctrinally speaking, Robert Gundry might as well be hired to *teach* at The Criswell College!

Regarding Gundry's fundamental error about the feeding of the 4,000 (which Dr. McCall addresses in Chapter 7), Dr. Cooper does not even attempt an answer.

Finally, Dr. Cooper seems to defend Gundry's stance on Replacement Theology. But if the Church has replaced Israel, even for the time-being, then Gundry's views contradict the school's stance on dispensational theology.

It is, however, Dr. Cooper's final statements in his letter that caused us greatest concern.

> I think I have tried to be fair in my assessment of these facts. As I stated to you in our meeting, I am no fan of Robert Gundry. At the same time I have to say that I cannot find convincing evidence that the textbook is heretical or anti-Semitic.

What a slap! After admitting that he (the Vice President and Provost of the college) wouldn't use the book based on the his knowledge of Robert Gundry personally, Dr. Cooper now feels that the book is all right to use on those "impressionable" freshmen whose first survey of the New Testament will be Robert Gundry's!

This change in attitude was remarkable—and disturbing! If The Criswell College would now defend this heresy and continue to use it to indoctrinate their pastors-to-be, then we felt no choice but to take action. Here's how I reported it to our readers in our June 1998 *Levitt Letter*:

> Realizing that the end of the term was May 14, I got our television crew together and in 24 hours we had finished a program on this appalling textbook. Twenty-four hours later, it was edited and post-produced, and 24 hours after that it was distributed nationally for airing on May 9-10. [It should be noted that we gave Dr. Cooper advanced notice of this taping, inviting him to come to our studio as our guest. He chose not to participate.]
>
> If these colleges continue to use this textbook, we will continue to run this program or a similar one periodically. We may call other theologians and academicians to help combat this problem. They won't be hard to find.
>
> The publisher of the textbook is Zondervan Publishing House. When I wrote for Zondervan in the '70s, it was extremely careful about Bible doctrine. Times seemed to have changed, or its philosophy has changed.

On June 24, 1998, Dr. Tom McCall and I sent the following letter to Dr. Richard C. Wells, president of The Criswell College:

> As you may know, we recently ran a TV program featuring a critique of the book by Robert H. Gundry, *A Survey of the New Testament*, and its widespread use in Christian schools, including The Criswell College. The problem is that it is replete with subtle anti-Jewish attitudes and interpretations of the Scriptures that gradually indoctrinate students against Jews and against Israel. Many times the authors and teachers

do this without realizing it, and would even vigorously deny that they have an anti-Jewish bias. The fruit of this subtle animosity toward the Jews, though, is very bitter and includes the following:

1. It results in coldness toward Jewish evangelism, which was a very high priority in the ministries of the two chief apostles, Peter and Paul.
2. It develops into an attitude of hostility toward Jewish believers in Christ.
3. It fosters a distorted view of Israel's place in God's plan in the past, present, and future.
4. It presents a skewed view concerning the nature and purpose of the church, especially the notions of Replacement Theology.
5. It produces an indifferent and sometimes hostile view toward the modern struggling state of Israel, an island of democracy in a sea of barbaric Muslim dictatorships. This is particularly galling because it is these same Muslim dictatorships that are today persecuting Christians in their countries on a horrific scale.
6. Finally, it results in an indifferent attitude toward the fate of the Jews suffering persecutions, such as the Holocaust and its aftermath, which continues up to the present.

How can a book on the New Testament cause so much harm and discord? It is by stealth and deception, sometimes knowingly, sometimes unintentionally. We have already reviewed many of the objectionable things about Gundry's book with you, but the following points highlight the major problems.

1. Whenever the Jews are referred to, it is usually with negative overtones, but when the Gentiles are mentioned, it is in terms of their nobility and eager faith. This shows an underlying anti-Jewish bias.
2. In order to establish the notion that Jesus Himself ministered to great masses of Gentiles, Gundry assumes by very faulty reasoning that the miracle of the feeding of the 4,000 was among Gentiles deep in the Decapolis area. The evidence, however, is that this miracle was also among Jews just as was the feeding of the 5,000.
3. Gundry implies that Christ's earthly ministry only to Israel was a flawed procedure at best, and perhaps even a mistake. This undermines the dispensational character of the Lord's ministry before His death and resurrection, and even attacks the deity of the Lord.
4. The book moves in the direction of teaching Replacement Theology, indicating that the Church has "replaced" Israel, "at least for the time being." Gundry claims to believe in the future of Israel, but his teaching blurs the dispensational distinctive between the time of Christ's teaching and the later establishment of the church.

We are concerned about these issues, not only because we are interested in Biblical truth, but also because we believe the Lord has given us a ministry to serve as monitors or watchdogs to warn Christians when they get involved in anti-Jewish writings and attitudes. We feel this textbook is a strong case in point, mainly because its use is so widespread in Christian halls of learning.

We would appreciate it if you would use your good offices to remove Gundry's book as a text in New Testament studies, and replace it with one more in line with the views of the founder, Dr. W. A. Criswell, and his excellent *Criswell Study Bible.* We understand you have personal knowledge that Dr. Gundry was himself expelled from the Evangelical Theological Society for his unorthodox views. Why should The Criswell College promote a text by an author who has been repudiated by his peers? Also, we understand that Zondervan Publishing House has become much less interested in doctrinal concerns since Pat Zondervan left. Why use a textbook publisher that has a reputation for moving away from sound doctrine?

It might be good if we could get together to discuss these issues at length. Also, would you be interested in being interviewed on the TV program about this matter? If so, when would you like to do this? Please let us know.

Thank you for your continuing concerns about these important Scriptural issues. We look forward to hearing from you soon.

We never did receive word from Dr. Wells or anyone else from The Criswell College about their desire to appear on our program to set the record straight.

In response to our letter, Dr. Wells sent us a reply one month later (now eight months since the issue was first brought to their attention) in which he defends Dr. Gundry and his book. Here are a few excerpts:

A Textbook Case

First on Gundry. As I indicated in our initial meeting, members of the Evangelical Theological Society (ETS) voted to remove Professor Gundry from membership some ten years ago. At issue was his use of form critical methods, which many members considered inconsistent with the ETS definition of biblical inerrancy. It should be noted, however, (1) that Gundry *did* not (and to my knowledge, *does* not) agree with that judgment, and (2) that the vote was not unanimous. In fairness then, Gundry was not "repudiated by his peers." Further, while in my judgment the ETS acted appropriately, we must be careful not to judge Gundry's views as "unorthodox" on the strength of a scholarly dispute over the definition of inerrancy, since the term "unorthodox" implies heresy. In short, Gundry may not be (probably is not) a strict inerrantist in the "Chicago Statement" sense; but that does not, in and of itself, mean that he is a heretic, nor of course that he harbors an anti-Jewish bias.

Really! Please re-read that last statement from Dr. Wells. Dr. Gundry, in his opinion, does not believe in the total inerrancy of the Bible! And now The Criswell College feels it their duty to defend the man and allow a book based on such views to be the first introduction to the New Testament? Does this not clearly show that Gundry's book, based on his errantist point of view, contradicts the statement of faith of The Criswell College, which upholds the total inerrancy of Scripture? He as much as contradicts Dr. Cooper's original opinion that the book does not go against their statement of faith. In fact, he goes on in this letter to admit that "it is unquestionably true that Gundry's eschatology differs from that which is stated in the Articles of Faith of The Criswell College." Let us remember that Gundry's book was not being used as merely as recommended reading in addition to a primary text on the New Testament. Gundry's book *was* the primary textbook, which means that the students were drilled in the facts contained in his book. In other words, these "impressionable" freshmen students were forming their initial and primary views on the New Testament Scriptures from an author who does not believe in inerrancy and who does not agree with the school's eschatology. What is there to defend here? The book is in error. The author has been proven to be in error *by a majority* of his peers.

Dr. Well's passionate defense that he has "reflected on and prayed over" this matter, while nonetheless approving the book for use as a teacher decides, shows the unwillingness of the school to take a stand against materials that are in error. This attitude reflects on the entire school and on the good name of that venerable Bible teacher, W. A. Criswell, for whom the school was named.

Finally, Dr. Wells implies that our ministry is trying to tear down The Criswell College:

> My brothers, it would be a great tragedy if a Christ-honoring, biblically-based, missions-hearted ministry such as The Criswell College, with a long history of support for Israel and an unwavering commitment to the same—if such a ministry should come under a cloud of suspicion in the minds of sincere Christian men and women who know nothing more about this work than what has been implied by broadcasts and letters of Zola Levitt Ministries.

Our goal from the beginning of this "battle" was merely to help a sister ministry from falling into error and passing that error onto its graduates, who become our future pastors and teachers. As far as being "biblically-based," I would question a school that allowed as a primary text, a book replete with biblical errors from an author who is convinced the Bible is not 100% error-free!

By August, not only had the problem with this book not improved, our ministry and I myself began to receive more personal attacks from the schools defending their use of Gundry's book, as I explained in this update:

> Sometimes a fellow just doesn't know what to write. I started out last November to point out to college administrators of my own denomination that they had inadvertently selected a bad textbook. They agreed with me completely and even gave me reasons for the book's errors. They indicated they would look carefully at the book and get back to me in good time. But six months passed, and then they pronounced the book flawless and refused to get rid of it.
>
> Now one of them is sending out a mean-spirited letter about me to those of you who write to The Criswell College. Having no real defense for this awful textbook, they undertake to attack the messenger.
>
> I am not uncomfortable at the university level. I spent ten years in institutions of higher learning, and I taught at three universities. I have known administrators and faculty members both good and bad my whole life. And I am used to being taken seriously. I'm familiar with only three people at The Criswell College. One of them, Dr. Paul Wolfe, the head of the Depart-

ment of New Testament Studies, was my student at Dallas Baptist University. He had become an ardent believer in Replacement Theology, my son Aaron determined in a three-hour interview. The second one is sending out the letter about me, and the third one, the president of the college, told me face-to-face that the author's theology was called unacceptable by a learned Bible society.

Let me say that the whole atmosphere of hostility makes me sad and very troubled. I thought I would be thanked for my effort. I am only criticizing a textbook, not a college or its administrators. This is not a personal matter. The book is patently wrong, and there is no way anyone can answer for its many errors without slipping into language that suggests a less than honest approach. "Spin control" has no place in Christian discourse. If The Criswell College was formed to teach the Bible, then the present administrators have forgotten what they came for.

I want to thank those of you who wrote to Criswell in regard to the textbook *A Survey of the New Testament, Third Edition*, by Robert H. Gundry. I know that you received letters from Dr. Lamar Cooper, the Executive Vice President of the college. He was the administrator Aaron and I dealt with, along with President Richard Wells, when we first reported the errors in the book last November. At that time, Dr. Cooper seemed to agree with us. He listened while Dr. Wells told me that author Gundry had been expelled from the Evangelical Theological Society because of his unacceptable theology. The issue was one especially precious to Baptists, Biblical inerrancy. Gundry's book gives ample evidence of his distrust of Scriptural veracity and even the deity of our Lord. A thesis of his is that the Messiah made a mistake in coming to the Jews and corrected it by turning to the Gentiles. Dr. Cooper himself deplored how Zondervan Publishing Company has deteriorated over the years, as an explanation of how such a book could come about. He assured me at that time that he would look carefully at the text and get back to me promptly.

But Dr. Cooper's reply to our readers' letters characterizes me as some kind of radical, running off half-cocked on a "crusade." He does not mention that Dr. Thomas S. McCall, a Baptist theologian of unquestioned knowledge and skill—ordained by W.A. Criswell himself—was also on our "A Textbook Case" television program. We came with two witnesses, as Scripture requires, and we presented our case. Dr. McCall, a Gentile Christian, certified that the book was anti-Semitic, anti-Israel, full of Replacement Theology, etc., etc.

A wise Christian told me recently that when Christians form big organizations, they often behave like big organizations, not like Christians. They become defensive and tricky. When told that cigarettes were bad for people, the tobacco companies called the accusations a "controversy." When I say that wrongheaded Bible is bad for students, the school calls it a "crusade." But I know that Gundry's awful textbook has been out since 1970 in three different editions, and thousands of pastors and laymen have been misguided by it. (In an upcoming letter, we will show how Gundry's theology doesn't even agree from edition to edition of his own book.) Why does a college use a textbook by an author it knows is badly qualified and in which the theology is so questionable? (Aaron's classroom teacher was disheartened and didn't want to use it, but was compelled to do so. He referred Aaron to Dr. Wolfe.) Well, I think it bears mentioning that the publisher, Stanley Gundry of Zondervan, is the brother of the author. Why does the college fight so hard to keep such a book? Cooper's letter cites that Zondervan "first published it while Pat Zondervan, a champion for truth, was still CEO of the publishing company." But Cooper does not go on to say that the company has since been sold and taken over by individuals he told me personally are doctrinally far less careful.

I have consulted more than one theologian on the author's positions. It turns out that Gundry debated with Dr. Thomas Ice on a radio program three months ago, and he defended the post-Tribulation Rapture position. That thinking, which would take the Church through the Tribulation period, runs counter to normal Baptist theology, to say nothing of Scripture itself. The entire idea of the imminence of the Rapture is simply done away with. It is hard to think of a more damaging teaching in the field of prophecy.

As to Cooper's statement that "the text makes no claims that could be labeled 'replacement theology'," I will again cite Gundry's *Third Edition*, page 161: "Matthew writes his gospel for the Church as the new chosen nation, which, at least for the time being, has replaced the old chosen nation of Israel." If that's not Replacement Theology, then words don't have meanings. Replacement Theology is usually found at liberal seminaries and the sort of denominations that dislike Israel and the Jews, not in a conservative, evangelical school. (My book *Broken Branches* explains this odious doctrine and how truly unbiblical it is.)

The anti-Semitism in the Gundry book is revealed in constant references to the Jewish people in gospel times as being faithless and treacherous, and the Gentile people as being noble and eager for faith. You almost have to read this offensive book to get the tenor of it, but I've had a lifetime of these subtle references to Jewish inferiority, and I have a very good ear for it. (More importantly, young students may not have as much sensitivity to these issues and are easily led astray.) Dr. McCall's letter to Dr. Wells, which will be appearing in our upcoming newsletter, will amplify this point.

As to the book being anti-Israel, one has only to consider the fact that first-century Israel is called Palestine throughout, almost without exception. The word Israel does not even appear in the index! In Gundry's mind, there was no such country. And yet, in the first century, no one in the world used the word Palestine for the whole country of Israel. The Bible certainly doesn't, not even once, not cover-to-cover, Old Testament or New. Dr. Cooper's letter to me of May 1st says that his "personal conviction" about the matter is that we should not "surrender" the "use of the name Palestine." Theologians use the term "surrender" to denote their holding fast to an important Biblical doctrine, as in "I will not surrender the deity of Christ," or "I will not surrender the imminence of the Rapture." But nobody should refuse to "surrender" what is patently unbiblical and wrong. Any Bible reader is certainly aware of the Scriptural inaccuracy and the political implications of saying Palestine when one means Israel.

Author Gundry's constant references to Jesus' "Palestinian disciples" seem engineered to play into today's politics. Hanan Ashrawi of the Palestinian Authority once declared, "Jesus was a Palestinian prophet born in Bethlehem in my country." The Palestinians should publish Gundry's book in Gaza. It would support their cause of making our Lord an Arab.

I know there are false teachers in the world, and I'm not naive about the difference between simple doctrinal disagreement and Biblical error. False teaching is a grave Biblical sin. Using the writing of an author like this on young people is like serving poisoned food in a school cafeteria.

Some big organizations listen to reason. In July, both CNN and *Time* magazine retracted a story after pressure from a number of sources. It seems they had their facts wrong. I can tell you that neither organization is very given to apologies. I have written to both on many occasions; they consider themselves next to perfect. But with expert testimony on the facts staring them in the face, they were able, with dignity, to back down. They even fired some high-ranking people. It is possible that on the subjects of Israel, anti-Semitism, Replacement Theology and the like, that my books, my 58 tours of Israel and my twenty years of television programs on these subjects might eventually persuade this college that my complaint is valid.

I really am sorry to have to trouble you, our audience, with this textbook matter; but after all, a generation of young people has been raised on wrong doctrine, and it is time that something is done. But it's discouraging work. We reported in our July newsletter that Southeast College of Lakeland, Florida, had informed a viewer of ours that they would discontinue its use of the book. I'm sorry to tell you that they sent a recent letter defending it with no better defense than that of The Criswell College. We will run the letter of the chairman of their Bible Department in our upcoming newsletter.

Listed below are the page numbers of Aaron's 49 complaints about the Gundry's book (*Third Edition*). They are grouped into six subject areas (inspiring Dr. Cooper to write that Aaron had "only 6" complaints). Know that I could find 490 more and Dr. McCall 4,900, I imagine.

- Replacement Theology: pages 117, 151, 161, 206, 258, 262, 265, 268, 279, 282, 295
- "Palestinian": pages 23, 78, 79, 147, 163
- Christianity and Roman Empire in harmony: 227, 238, 239, 240, 243, 247, 248, 298, 303
- Hellenism: pages 215, 216, 240, 259, 285, 304
- Anti-Semitism: pages 219, 286, 297, 329
- Contradiction of Jesus' speech and action: pages 137, 186-7

The last letter from The Criswell College which we cite for you is dated September 3, 1998 and written to a concerned viewer from Florida. Rather than deal with the *un*biblical views of and statements in Gundry's book, Dr. Wells sought to disparage our attempts at exposing these errors.

Let me say that there is a great deal more at issue here than either the timeliness of our response, or even criticisms against the Gundry book. Scripture is very clear that, even in cases of proven wrongdoing—which is most assuredly not the case here—but *even in such cases*, Christians have no justification for accusing Christian brothers publicly. Even if a brother is caught in a fault, Paul declares, those who are spiritual are to restore him in meekness and humility (Gal. 6:1). The Lord requires attempts at private resolution, then two or three witnesses, then, if need by, the church (Matt. 18:15-17). But "the church" is not a nationwide television audience nor a ministry database. My brother, I must speak the truth in love. Scripture gives no warrant at all for the public airing of accusations. Criticisms should be to us or to the First Baptist Church of Dallas,

Texas, under whose authority we minister.

Mr. Levitt has a large media apparatus at his disposal; and we have no defense except to answer those who write. But the Scripture warns that "He who gives an answer before he hears, it is folly and shame to him" (Prov. 18:13). My prayerful hope is that, for the sake of Christ, you will judge The Criswell College on the basis of knowledge, not innuendo.

A couple of points of interest in Dr. Well's letter to this concerned Christian. First, you can see from the above progression of correspondence that we, in fact, began this process privately, first meeting in December 1997. We were put off again and again, letter after letter, meeting after meeting, only to have the college admit that Robert H. Gundry's views contradicted the statement of faith of The Criswell College, and that, despite this fact, the college would still allow the textbook to be used. Secondly, we gave Dr. Wells and Dr. Cooper ample opportunities to use our "large media apparatus" to voice their side of the issue; they chose not to do so. And finally, note that Dr. Wells, the president of The Criswell College, states that the college operates "under the authority" of the First Baptist Church of Dallas. Interestingly, this contradicts the statement of the pastor of First Baptist Church, who vehemently denied that the Church had any governing authority over the college radio station KCBI (see Chapter 3).

The Criswell College gave us quite a battle and to my knowledge they are still using the textbook full bore. There's just nothing more we can do and I simply don't understand it. I rather suspect that they may get it at a bargain price since the author's brother is the editor for the Zondervan Publishing House, but I don't know that for a fact. I am still stymied as to why they would defend a textbook of this sort so vehemently and refuse to put it aside even after admitting it was contrary to their own articles of faith.

We seem to end at loggerheads with our side saying that the book is unacceptable and their side claiming that while not perfect, the book is still useable. Frankly, the only middle ground I can imagine is that Dr. McCall and I, having long careers in Jewish evangelism, have much more sensitivity to anti-Semitism and Replacement Theology than that of the Gentile professors who defend this book. I have found that to be true in every one of our battles. I sincerely believe these professors and presidents of seminaries when they say they are not anti-Semitic and yet their actions simply write off the Chosen People and the Promised Land at every turn. It may be they simply don't realize the implications of what they do and what they teach since they have so long been members of what they think of as purely a Gentile Christian Church. In my travels, I have verified that the Church is probably equal in Jews and Gentiles *per capita* and probably God has been saving people in this proportion all the way since Pentecost. In view of the fact that American Jewish adults occur about every one in 200 people in our society, we would find one in 200 people in the Christian church to be Jewish on the average. I have verified this over 30 years of ministry. In Israel, close to 100% of the Messianic church members are Jewish.

With all of that said and with the concessions that I made above, I still very sincerely feel that the seminaries are sliding down a slippery slope into liberal doctrine and they are not doing it for reasons of anti-Jewishness or anti-Semitism, but for money, as I detail in Part Two regarding Moody Bible Institute.

Obviously broadening doctrines is a way of taking in more students. Unfortunately, the Lord said, "The way is narrow."

Chapter 6
Gundry Responds ♦

We have now received letters from the author, Robert H. Gundry, and Zondervan Publishing House attempting to defend their textbook, *A Survey of the New Testament, Third Edition*. Please note that they accuse Zola and me of making charges that are unfounded, misleading and irresponsible; they also accuse you of writing letters to them in ignorance, without having read the textbook yourselves.

I will attempt to answer the main points Dr. Gundry raises in response to our complaints in letters, newsletters and the TV program.

There are two points that should be kept in mind in all of this debate. One is that Dr. Gundry was expelled out of the Evangelical Theological Society because of his unorthodox views on the iner-

---

♦ When our ministry office received correspondence from Dr. Robert Gundry defending his textbook, I asked Dr. Tom McCall, our theologian, to respond point by point. He does so here with some introductory comments to our readers. This "theological battle" was originally printed in the August 1998

rancy of Scripture, a fact that is not mentioned in his biographical descriptions. Why should we educate our future pastors and Christian leaders with a textbook by an author who has been so repudiated by his evangelical peers? The other is that Dr. Gundry is one of the leading proponents of the post-Tribulation Rapture viewpoint, and has written several books on the subject. Many of the schools that are using his New Testament textbook were founded on the conviction that the Lord will return for the church before the Tribulation with a pre-Trib Rapture. Why should these schools use as a textbook a New Testament survey book by an author who promotes an eschatological view contrary to that on which the schools were founded?

In the following discussion, I mean no disrespect by referring to Dr. Gundry as simply Gundry. This is common in theological discourse. I have responded below to each of the paragraphs in Gundry's letter.

Dr. Gundry: You said the book is "anti-Israel" and "anti-Semitic" and it "demeans" and "defames" the Jewish people. Your senior theological advisor, Dr. Thomas S. McCall, added, "Every time he [Gundry] mentions the Gentiles, they're noble-minded, high-minded, and full of faith" whereas the Jews are "the worst things that ever happened." You also spoke of "those murderous Jews we read about" in the book, and described Paul the Pharisee as "not rotten at all," in contrast to my description of the Pharisees.

These accusations need a double answer. First, Paul himself described his Phariseeism as "dung" (Philippians 3:8). No less an authority than Jesus issued a long series of woes against the scribes and Pharisees for their hypocrisy (Matt. 23), not to detail other criticisms (the parable of the Pharisee and publican, for example). Peter, himself a Jew, told the "men of Israel" that they had taken Jesus "by lawless hands" and "put him to death" (Acts 2:23). So

Stephen called them "murderers" (Acts 7:52), and Paul wrote that "wrath has come upon them ['the Jews'] to the uttermost" (1 Thessalonians 2:14-16; compare the frequently derogatory use of "the Jews" in John's gospel—5:16, to take but one example, "the Jews persecuted Jesus, and sought to kill him"). These passages do not excuse anti-Semitism, and Gentiles bear an equal load of guilt for Jesus' death; but if I had wanted to defame the Jews in SNT, I would have highlighted a passage like the Thessalonian one. I did not even mention it.

Dr. McCall: Gentiles have a problem writing about the condemnations of the Jewish people that are contained in both the Old and New Testaments. The tendency is for us to fall into the trap of thinking that God is more angry with Israel than He is with the Gentile nations. This is a terrible fallacy. In comparison, the Lord has much more condemnation against the nations of the world than against His own people. Furthermore, He reserves the greatest condemnation against those nations and individual Gentiles who abuse His Chosen People. We must maintain that perspective in all our pronouncements and writings. Of course, when individual Jews and Gentiles receive Christ, there is equal blessing and salvation for both.

Dr. Gundry: Second, although my book emphasizes the conversion of many Gentiles, as the New Testament does, it also describes in lurid detail the degeneracy of Gentile morals, entertainment, and pagan religion (pages 50-51, 56-62) and notes that many Gentiles were attracted to the Jewish religion because of its superior morals and theology (page 73). Additional note is taken that "in Abraham's descendants all the families of the earth will be blessed" (page 304). I dare say that your viewers and readers would never guess from your presentations that Jewish-favorable and Gentile-critical material appears in my book.

Dr. McCall: While Gundry has praise for the superior morals and theology of the "Jewish religion," he has scant appreciation for the Jewish people themselves, who were the repository of the Word of God and the Messianic hope. Although there are some complimentary passages about the Jews, the tenor of the book as a whole is uncomplimentary of the Jewish people, and fails to recognize the great minority of Jews who received Jesus, His teaching, and His ministry.

Dr. Gundry: Next, you accused me of "trying to leave out the Jews" with my interpretation of Matt. 15:31, "And they glorified the God of Israel," as a reference to Gentiles' glorification of Israel's God (page 187). One might have thought you would regard it as a compliment to Jews that Gentiles would be glorifying the God of Israel. No matter, though; it would not bother me in the least if Jews were doing the glorifying; and of course I recognize that they too, could use the phrase, "the God of Israel" (as they do in Psalms 41:13; 106:48; Luke 1:68, Acts 13:17). But these are the editorial words of Matthew, not directly quoted words of the multitude; and although Jesus had said, "I was not sent except to the lost sheep of the house of Israel" (Matt. 15:24), he did in fact minister to the Gentile woman who had just come to him, as he had also ministered to the Gentile centurion who had come to him earlier (Matt. 8:5-13), so that it does not seem a "preposterous idea" (your phrase) that the multitudes who came to him and glorified the God of Israel should be seen as Gentiles. Note well that Jesus did not go to them; they came to him, just as the centurion and the woman had done (Matt. 8:5; 15:22, 30).

Dr. McCall: The point about Matt. 15:31, "And they glorified the God of Israel," is that, in the book, Gundry takes this as proof that these people were Gentiles, with no further explanation. Gundry says in the letter that "it would not bother me in the least if Jews were doing the glorifying." But that would undermine his whole argument that Christ was now turning away from the Jews to the Gentiles. The assumption that this was a large group of Gentiles is critical to his position. We show that there is no bona fide reason to assume that these were anything other than Israelites with whom the Lord was dealing all along.

Dr. Gundry: To counteract my statement that the multitudes "represent the great mass of Gentiles who are flocking into the church of Matthew's time," Dr. McCall asserted, "There was no Church in Matthew's time; Jesus was presenting the kingdom to his people Israel." But my verb, "represents," shows that "Matthew's time" was the time of his writing, when there most certainly was a church already in existence. Dr. McCall's assertion would have been correct only if "Matthew's time" had meant the lifetime of Jesus. It does not.

Dr. McCall: Concerning "Matthew's time," the natural assumption is that Gundry is referring to the time Matthew is writing about, during the earthly ministry of our Lord. With regard to tense, in the textbook he states, "they represent the great mass of Gentiles who are flocking into the church of Matthew's time." If he intended it to mean the time after the beginning of the Church Age, he should have clarified this by using the future tense, such as "the great mass of Gentiles who will later flock into the church at the time Matthew wrote his gospel." Nevertheless, there was no great mass of Gentiles involved in the ministry of our Lord, before His death, resurrection and ascension, as I have endeavored to explain above.

Dr. Gundry: Contrary to Dr. McCall's further argument, you will not find in SNT any statement to the effect that for the purpose of feeding the multitude of 4,000 Jesus ventured "deep into this Gentile area of Decapolis" or "into the heart of Decapolis." But since Dr. McCall has brought up the matter, I observe that though he correctly translates *horion* with "border," he fails to note that in Mark 7:31, where the word occurs in a parallel to the Matthean passage under discussion, the word occurs in the plural, with a preceding phrase, *ana meson* (literally, "up the middle"), that produces the meaning, "between the borders of Decapolis," that is, "in the middle of Decapolis." Matthew 13:25 uses the same preceding phrase for the sowing of tares "between," that is, "in the middle of," wheat. Furthermore, Dr. McCall errs to argue simplistically that Galilee was Jewish, so that a Galilean setting would guarantee the Jewishness of a crowd. In fact, the population of Galilee was mixed. Why, within several miles, easy walking distance, of Jesus' hometown of Nazareth in Galilee lay a major Gentile city, Sepphoris. Archaeologists have been excavating it for some years now (compare Matt. 4:15: "Galilee of the Gentiles").

Dr. McCall: With regard to the translation of *ana meson ton horion Decapolis*, Gundry concludes that it means, "in the middle of Decapolis." However, it literally means, "in the midst of the border of Decapolis." The idea is that Jesus came to the northern border of Decapolis, probably not far from the Jewish town of Gamla, about midway between the Sea of Galilee and the eastern boundary. My two articles about the feeding of the 4,000 (*Levitt Letter*, July and August issues) go into this matter in considerable detail, and I would refer the reader to those articles.

Dr. Gundry: But this disagreement over the multitude of 4,000 has little or no theological significance. For even under my view that they prefigure the later influx of Gentiles into the church, Jesus still aimed his ministry toward the Jews. Whether few or many,

Gundry Responds

Gentiles who benefited from it formed exceptions. Even Dr. McCall admits Gentile exceptions that proved the Jewish rule. He limits those exceptions to isolated individuals, however, so as to rule out the multitude; and he quotes Jesus' instruction to the disciples that they not minister to Gentiles and Samaritans (Matt. 10:5). But John 4 tells us that Jesus "must needs go through Samaria," that he took the initiative in ministering there to a Samaritan woman, and that "many" of the Samaritans "believed because of his own word" in addition to that of the woman (verses 4, 7, 39-42). No matter what Dr. McCall says, then, non-Jewish exceptions to the Jewish thrust of Jesus' ministry cannot be limited to isolated individuals.

Dr. McCall: Gundry states in his letter that "this disagreement over the multitude of 4,000 has little or no theological significance," even though in the text he bases most of his argument for the Gentile ministry of Christ on that premise. Then he attempts to prove his thesis on the basis of the Lord's ministry to the Samaritans in John 4, an argument he did not use in the text. The Samaritans, though, are a special case. They are not considered Gentiles, but rather apostate and corrupted Israelites. After all, the Samaritan woman said "our father, Jacob" gave them the well. She considered herself an Israelite. After Pentecost, Peter and Phillip had a ministry in Samaria in Acts 8, and this was not considered out of the ordinary, because the Samaritans were, at least partially, Jews. It was not until Peter ministered to full Gentiles (the house of Cornelius), that there was an uproar about the Gospel going outside the realm of the Jewish people. Thus, it is not what I say, but the Scriptures say that the rule of Jesus' restricted ministry to Israel was broken only by rare individual exceptions.

Dr. Gundry: Your TV presentation in June called it an "implication" of my view that "God made a mistake" by sending Jesus

103

to the Jews if his main purpose had to do with Gentiles. Your August newsletter now calls it my "thesis" that "the Messiah made a mistake in coming to the Jews and corrected it by turning to the Gentiles." In fact, nowhere does SNT state or imply that the Jewish mission was a divine or messianic mistake. Ironically, it is non-dispensationalists who usually charge dispensationalists like you and Dr. McCall with implying such a mistake in that God and the Messiah should have known the Jewish nation would reject an offer of the kingdom, and therefore should have gone directly to the Gentiles instead of introducing the church only as a stopgap at the last moment. Not that I level this charge. I do not; for though I hold to the historic Christian view of a post-Tribulational Rapture of the church (for my reasons, see *First the Antichrist* [Grand Rapids: Baker, 1977]), I join you and other dispensationalists in seeing an offer of the kingdom to the Jews during Jesus' earthly ministry (see SNT, pages 114-115: "Through his preaching, Jesus brought God's rule to the Jews").

Dr. McCall: Gundry does not really answer our charge that he appears to consider the ministry of Christ among the Jews a mistake. The whole tenor of the book is that the Lord was deeply distressed by the attitude of the Jews, and was greatly encouraged by His supposed reception among the Gentiles during His earthly ministry. It is the implications of this view that are so devastating. It implies (even if it does not clearly state) that the Lord had made a dreadful mistake in spending so much of His time among the Jews, when He could have had a much more effective ministry among the Gentiles. If the Lord made such a mistake, it would imply that He was merely human and not deity in the flesh. We are not claiming that Gundry flatly denies the deity of Christ, but that the logical conclusions of some of his positions about the ministry of the Lord would lead in that direction.

104

Gundry Responds

Dr. Gundry: You say that I subscribe to "Replacement Theology," which you define as the view that "God's through with the Jews. God's fed up. He's had enough." Then you cite my statement, "Matthew writes his gospel for the church as the new chosen nation, which at least for the time being has replaced the old chosen nation of Israel" (page 161). But my phrase "at least for the time being" shows that I do not believe God is through with the Jews. This belief should be clear also from my references to "the renewal of Israel" (page 191, concerning Matt. 19:28) and to the future repentance of the Jews, so that "all Israel will be saved, that is, those Jews who are still living at the return of Christ.... Therefore Gentile believers should not self-righteously exalt themselves over Jewish believers..." (page 386, concerning Romans 9-11, the very passage to which you and Dr. McCall appealed with the same understanding as mine; and see page 475 for my premillennialism). As regards the Jews' temporary replacement by the church (which contains a remnant of believing Jews as well as a mass of believing Gentiles), my language echoes Matt. 21:43 ("the kingdom of God will be taken from you and given to a nation bearing the fruits of it") and Romans 11:11-36 (where Paul writes about the Jews "falling," "being cast away," "broken off," "not being spared," and "being hardened in part...until the fullness of the Gentiles has come in").

Dr. McCall: In his letter, Gundry states that he does not subscribe to Replacement Theology, because he states in his book that the church has replaced Israel "at least for the time being." Thus, he says, the church's replacement of Israel is only temporary, and there is a future for Israel. This is not as bad as the standard Replacement Theology, but it is still too much. The church has not replaced Israel at all; Israel is still in a covenantal relationship with God, which has not been changed. The church has been brought in for this current age to accomplish the Lord's purposes as the Bride of Christ. However, the church is not Israel, and it has not replaced Israel.

Dr. Gundry: Whether or not Luke was a Gentile does not matter a great deal, as Dr. McCall seemed to recognize on your TV program in June; but I was surprised that neither you nor he tried to explain why in Colossians 4:7-15 Paul does not mention Luke until after he has mentioned others whom he described as his "only fellow workers...who are of the circumcision." Since I cited this passage (page 206), I did not simply "assume" Luke's being a Gentile, as Dr. McCall asserted. I forgo other arguments on this relatively minor point, but it strains the imagination for you to deduce that someone is anti-Jewish for thinking that Luke was probably a Gentile. I am sure you have seen, indeed experienced, real anti-Semitism, so that it puzzles me why you cannot distinguish it from the question of Luke's ethnicity.

Dr. McCall: Gundry says that the ethnicity of Luke does not matter. However, if Luke was a Gentile, it would mean that God had reversed His policy of using only Jews to write revealed Scripture:

> What advantage then hath the Jew? Or what profit is there of circumcision? Much every way: chiefly, because that unto them were committed the oracles of God." (Rom. 3:1-2)

This is significant because Luke wrote more pages of the New Testament than any other writer. Anyone who believes that God broke His standard rule of using only Jews to write Scripture has the burden of proof on him. The answer to the Colossians passage and the arguments for Luke being a Jew are more fully developed in my previous article, "Was Luke a Gentile?" [March 1996 *Levitt*

Gundry Responds

Letter; available from our ministry]

Dr. Gundry: You called me to account for saying that Peter had to "defend himself against parochially minded Jewish believers in Jerusalem who criticize his going to Gentiles" (page 308), and you explained that "naturally these Jewish believers were questioning of Peter because they had never seen Gentile salvation before." Were you forgetting that Jesus had earlier given the Great Commission to make disciples of all the nations?

Dr. McCall: Gundry does not seem to comprehend how revolutionary the idea of bringing the Gospel to the Gentiles was to the Israeli church. The leaders of the first-century church in Israel—Peter and James—were simply not prepared, at first, for an influx of uncircumcised Gentiles into the body of the Messiah. They were not prepared by anything Christ did in His earthly ministry or by the Great Commission. They had to be carefully taught by special revelation and enlightenment before they could accept that the Lord was doing this new work as the Church Age began.

Dr. Gundry: You are correct; the index to SNT contains no entry for "Israel." But neither does it for "Gentiles" (yet you claim that the book has a pro-Gentile bias) or even for "Jesus" (yet you could hardly accuse the book of attacking Jesus). Obviously, the index is selective and not intended as a barometer of importance and unimportance. Who would say that "Albinus" is important just because it, or he, appears in the index?

Dr. McCall: The point about Israel in the index is that the term Israel is rarely used in the body of his textbook, much less than in the New Testament itself. It seems very strange that the ministry of the One who came to the lost sheep of the house of Israel, is described in a textbook on the New Testament with little reference to Israel.

Battles with Seminaries: Defending Israel

Dr. Gundry: As to the use of "Palestine" and "Palestinian," we all know that words mean what they mean according to current usage, not according to their derivation. Your use of "January" does not imply that you believe in the god Janus, after whom the month was named. "Prevent" does not mean "precede" any more, as it did in the King James Version of 1611 at 1 Thessalonians 4:15. So "Palestine" does not refer any more to the land of the Philistines. The map-makers who are responsible for the title, "Palestine in the Time of Jesus," are themselves Israelis. They hold the copyright, including the title against which you objected. Will you call them anti-Israel and anti-Semitic?

Dr. McCall: It is true that the term Palestine has entered into Biblical maps as well as textbooks, but it should be recognized that the term was never used in the New Testament, and that it was coined much later by the anti-Christian and anti-Jewish pagan Emperor Hadrian. He wanted to erase the memory of Jerusalem, Jesus and Israel from the face of the earth, after suppressing the Second Jewish War for Independence in 135 AD. To accomplish this purpose, he used the name of the ancient enemies of Israel, the pagan Philistines, and changed the name of the land to Palestine. Should we Christians participate in this attempt to obfuscate the name of Israel? It does not matter to Gundry, who is quite prepared to go with the flow.

Dr. Gundry: Finally, your latest newsletter attributes to me "distrust of scriptural veracity and even the deity of our Lord." Untrue! I both believe in the veracity of Scripture and teach its veracity (see pages 175 and 416 of SNT). The same goes for Jesus' deity (for example, see the statement on page 262 that the preincarnate Logos, or Christ, "shared God's own identity").

Dr. McCall: Gundry may believe in the veracity of the Scriptures and the deity of our Lord, but the logical extension of much that he teaches in his text would lead us to question the Scriptures and even the infallibility of Christ. But don't take our word on this. As we stated above, the Evangelical Theological Society considered Gundry's views about the Scripture to be unorthodox and expelled him from their membership. This alone should give us pause about using his textbook.

Dr. Gundry: To counter your claim that the *Third Edition* of SNT marks a theological deterioration from earlier editions, all my references to the book in refutation of your accusations have come from the allegedly corrupt *Third Edition*. I have no intention of prolonging this discussion beyond the current communication, nor do I pretend that you and I agree on every jot and tittle (though I suspect we agree on more that you think, and certainly on the major truths of the Christian faith). But in the interests of fairness and accuracy, you would do yourself a great honor, and me a great courtesy, to publish this open letter uncut and unedited.

Dr. McCall: It is remarkable that there has been a decided shift in viewpoint from the relatively mild first edition of Gundry's book to the *Third Edition*. He does not deny the changes, but merely states that he uses quotations from the *Third Edition* to respond to our complaints. The problem is that the later edition reflects a much stronger bias against Israel, a stronger insistence on a pre-Pentecost massive Gentile ministry by the Lord, and a partial embracing of Replacement Theology. The movements in these directions are symptomatic of the gradual decline in doctrinal accuracy from the first edition to the last.

It is my prayer that this discussion will help our readers understand the issues we are addressing, will draw them closer to the Lord, and will enable all of us to edify the church and proclaim the gospel of Christ "to the Jew first and also to the Gentile" (Rom. 1:16).

Chapter 7
The Feeding of the 4,000 —
Were They Gentiles? ✦

by Thomas S. McCall, Th.D.

There is a growing revisionist opinion among New Testament scholars that the second miraculous feeding (the 4,000) was done by the Lord deep in the Decapolis region, so that His ministry on this occasion was predominantly among Gentiles. Both Matthew and Mark describe the event as separate and apart from the feeding of the 5,000 at an earlier time.

Was Jesus on the border or deep in the region of Decapolis?

Mark especially gives the location of the event as having occurred in "the midst of the borders of Decapolis" (Mark 7:31, ASV),

---

✦ A compilation of two articles that originally appeared in the July and August 1998 *Levitt Letters.*

which suggest that it was on the fringes of the Decapolis area on the east side of the Sea of Galilee and the Jordan River. Other translations render it "within the region of Decapolis" (NASB) and in "the midst of the region of Decapolis" (NKJV), and suggest that the miracle was deep within the Decapolis area. How one translates this passage, and the location of the feeding of the 4,000, makes a lot of difference in understanding how broad the ministry of Christ was among Gentiles. Several commentaries indicate that Jesus and His disciples had gone far into the Decapolis region and were surrounded by Gentile cities.

What is the Decapolis?

Decapolis (literally, "10 cities") was primarily on the Golan Heights and on the east side of the Jordan River in the area that is now part of the Kingdom of Jordan. It was populated by Gentiles in the time of our Lord, and was largely pagan in religious practice. They were cities of Greco-Roman culture. It is so described in *The International Standard Bible Encyclopedia*, II, p. 815 under "Decapolis":

> The name given to the region occupied by a league of ten cities (Mt 4:25; Mk 5:20; 7:31). The Greek inhabitants were never on good terms with the Jews; and the herd of swine (Mk 5:11ff) indicates contempt for what was probably regarded as Jewish prejudice.

The revisionist commentaries would have us believe that Jesus ventured deep into this Gentile area of Decapolis so that He could have a broader ministry among the Gentiles. They see this as a harbinger of the great Gentile influx later as the apostles preached throughout the Roman empire. For instance, Robert H. Gundry in

The Feeding of the 4,000

A Survey of the New Testament (p. 187) assumes that the feeding of the 4,000 was a major accomplishment in the ministry of the Lord among the Gentiles:

> Read Matt. 15:21-28. "And they glorified the God of Israel" (15:31) shows that the four thousand whom Jesus now feeds are Gentiles. Together then with the preceding Gentile woman and, earlier, the centurion and the Magi, they represent the great mass of Gentiles who are flocking into the church of Matthew's time.

The only argument Gundry gives that the 4,000 were Gentiles is that they glorified the God of Israel. That logic makes no sense at all. Whom do Jews glorify when they read the Torah in the synagogues? To say that one has to be a Gentile to glorify the God of Israel is devoid of all reason. Nevertheless, he argues that the Syrophonecian woman, the centurion in Capernaum, and the Magi at the birth of Jesus combine with the 4,000 who were fed miraculously to constitute a great mass of Gentiles involved in Jesus' ministry. If you didn't have the 4,000, you would only have the five Gentile exceptions (but the three Magi might also have been Jews). Gundry and his revisionist colleagues must go to some lengths, then, to attempt to prove that the 4,000 were Gentiles. The facts, however, simply do not bear out this contention.

Jesus' rule of ministering only to Israel

If the 4,000 who were fed by the Lord were Gentiles, Jesus would have been departing from His announced rule that His ministry was only to Israel:

But go rather to the lost sheep of the house of Israel (Matt. 10:6);

But he answered and said, I am not sent but unto the lost sheep of the house of Israel (Matt. 15:24).

This rule had only the individual exceptions mentioned above, which proved the rule. Christ's entire earthly ministry was restricted to the Jewish people. There is no reason to believe that the 4,000 were any different from the 5,000 fed before. They also were Jewish people from the Sea of Galilee area who came to hear the Master.

The Meaning of "orion"

If the 4,000 were Jews, where was it that Jesus fed them? What was the site of this second spectacular and miraculous feeding? A closer reading of the Gospels shows that the text states that He was by the Sea of Galilee "in the midst of the border [or *orion*] of Decapolis." That is, He was near the Decapolis border close to the Sea of Galilee. Much hinges on the translation of the Greek term *orion*. Some try to translate it broadly as referring to a "region or district." However, one of the standards in Greek translation is *A Manual Greek Lexicon of the New Testament*, by G. Abbott-Smith. This manual has the following entry on the word on page 323: *orion*, -ou, to (*oros*, a boundary), [in LXX chiefly for] a boundary, bound; chiefly in pl., and so always in NT." Thus, the word is derived from *oros*, which means "mountain," a frequent boundary between geographical regions. It refers to a limit, a boundary or border of an area. Some try to make this mean that Jesus went into the heart of Decapolis, but what the word indicates is that He came to the border of Decapolis, not into the region.

It was also a "desert" area, and not close to any supply of food. All of these descriptions would put the site in the Jewish area of the Tetrarchy of Phillip near the Sea of Galilee, and north of the hill where Decapolis began. Jesus further indicates that it was within walking distance of their homes, but they needed to be fed in order to have the strength to make their way home. There is nothing to suggest that they were Gentiles. This whole area north of the Decapolis border was Jewish. The only town that had Gentiles in it was Julius, a pagan town not far from Bethsaida, close to where the Jordan River enters the Sea of Galilee. The map on page 213 shows where the Tetrarchy of Phillip and the Decapolis border is located, and the approximate locations of the two miraculous feedings.

The weight of evidence is that the location of the feeding of the 4,000 was in the Tetrarchy of Phillip just north of its border with the Decapolis, perhaps not far from the mountain town of Gamala, which became famous as "the Masada of the north" during the war Israel had against Rome later in the first century. It was far enough away from the shore of the Sea of Galilee that it would be considered a desert area, but close enough so that the Lord could go conveniently from there to the shore and take the boat to the other side.

Did Jesus visit Decapolis?

In our previous article, we explored the question of whether the Lord massively violated His announced rule of ministering only to Israel in His pre-death ministry, by going deep into the Decapolis area and feeding 4,000 Gentiles, as some revisionist commentaries suggest. We discovered that the terms used about Jesus going to the "border" of Decapolis will not allow for the idea of His going deep into the Decapolis region. In this article, we continue to explore this question. Did Jesus ever venture into Decapolis? If so, how far, and with what results? Also, what evidence, if any, is there in the Books of Acts that the Apostles were aware of any extensive Gentile ministry by the Lord before His death and resurrection? I believe the Scriptures answer these questions conclusively.

Did Jesus Ever Go to the Decapolis? Did Jesus ever venture into the Decapolis? Perhaps one time He came close, but we have no indication He ever ministered there to any great extent. There was one time when He may have stepped on the border of Decapolis near the Sea of Galilee, which was the hill just north of Gerasa (currently called Kursi). It is a hill that practically runs into the lake, and made a natural boundary between Decapolis on the south, and the Tetrarchy of Phillip on the north. Gerasa was in Decapolis. If one visits the Sea of Galilee, the location of Gerasa (Kursi) is clear. It sits in a valley made by a river that goes between the border hill on the north and the hills of the Golan Heights on the south.

The International Standard Bible Encyclopedia, II, pg. 1217, explains the unique characteristics of Gerasa:

> The town itself is not named in Scripture, and is referred to only in the expression, "country of the Gerasenes".... This describes the district in which Christ met and healed the demoniac from the tombs, where also took place the destruction of the swine. It was on the eastern shore of the Sea of Galilee, and must have been a locality where the steep edges of the Bashan plateau drop close upon

the brink of the lake. This condition is fulfilled only by the district immediately South of Wady Semak. . . Here the slopes descend swiftly almost into the sea, and animals, once started on the downward run, could not avoid plunging into the depths.

The occasion of our Lord's going to the hill bordering on Decapolis was when He healed the demoniac by casting out the demons and sending them into the pigs on the hill. Mark and Luke present essentially the same story:

And they came over unto the other side of the sea, into the country of the Gadarenes. And when he was come out of the ship, immediately there met him out of the tombs a man with an unclean spirit (Mark 5:1-2).

Matthew tells the same story, but includes the fact that there were two demoniacs:

And when he was come to the other side into the country of the Gergesenes, there met him two possessed with devils, coming out of the tombs, exceeding fierce, so that no man might pass by that way (Matt. 8:28).

Mark and Luke may not have mentioned the second one because the first was the one who asked to come with the Lord and then proceeded to testify of what the Lord had done for him among his own people.

These pigs were owned by the Gentile farmers of Gerasa (Kursi), and the demon-possessed pigs promptly ran down the hill into the Sea of Galilee and drowned. By the way, this is the only hill around the Sea of Galilee that juts right out to the shore, where this kind of event could occur. When the citizens of Gerasa heard what had happened, they came up the hill to ask Christ to leave—immediately. This was no outpouring of acceptance of the Lord by the Gentile inhabitants. These Gentiles of Decapolis thought Jesus was a menace to their way of life, and they wanted to be rid of Him. Thus, the only time Christ ventured toward Decapolis, it resulted in His being rejected by the Gentile inhabitants. It appears that He never had any contact with Decapolis again.

Was Peter aware of a broad Gentile ministry by Jesus? Not only does the wording in the Gospels preclude the idea that Jesus had a broad ministry in Decapolis, the later acts and arguments of the Apostles show that they had no background whatever for anything like a broad ministry among the Gentiles. Peter was astonished when the Centurion Cornelius of Caesarea received the Lord and was baptized by the Holy Spirit into the body of Christ. The other Apostles at the Jerusalem Conference were similarly astonished at the way Gentiles were receiving the same blessing Jews were receiving through faith in the Messiah. They had to have a specially convened meeting to determine if the Scriptures allowed for this kind of activity among the Gentiles.

If Jesus had already had a broad ministry among Gentiles in Decapolis and other areas, why were the Apostles surprised by what happened in Acts? Why didn't Peter remember the 4,000 Decapolis Gentiles Jesus ministered to and fed, if that is what really happened? Why didn't Peter use this event as an argument at the Jerusalem Conference when the question of Gentile salvation was raised? If the Lord Himself had ministered broadly among the Gentiles in Decapolis, this would have been a powerful argument when Peter explained to the other Apostles about his own ministry with Cornelius, and when Paul was urging the full acceptance of Gentile Christians at the Jerusalem Conference. The fact is, Peter never saw the Lord minister to masses of Gentile, in Decapolis or anywhere else.

Actually, when a group of Greek Gentiles came to see Jesus, He declined to give them an audience, saying that He had to die before He could have a fruitful ministry among the Gentiles (see paragraph headings and notes in the *New Scofield Reference Edition*, John 12:20ff): "Verily, verily, I say unto you, Except a corn of wheat fall into the ground and die, it abideth alone: but if it die, it bringeth forth much fruit" (John 12:24). Thus, until His death and resurrection, He restricted His ministry to His own Jewish people.

Some revisionist commentators have an agenda to show that Jesus had a massive outreach among Gentiles in His earthly ministry. If they can establish this, it will help them demolish the dispensational distinctives that exist before and after the death, burial and resurrection of our Lord. Their purpose is to show that Church Age concepts and the broad inclusion of Gentiles was something already instituted in the ministry of Christ before the cross. They also want to show that Jesus actually preferred ministry among the Gentiles in contrast with the difficulties He was having among the Jewish people. There is an undercurrent of anti-Jewish attitude in all of these commentaries and revisionist textbooks.

The only possible place these revisionists have to get large numbers of Gentiles into the ministry of the Lord is in this episode of the feeding of the 4,000. By twisting the wording around, they attempt to show that Jesus went into the heart of the Gentile region of Decapolis, preached to and healed large numbers of pagans, and concluded His ministry there with the miraculous feeding.

Battles with Seminaries: Defending Israel

The text of the New Testament simply does not support those views. Jesus repeatedly said that His ministry before His sacrificial death was limited to the people of Israel. Whenever there was an individual exception to this general rule, it was clearly and unequivocally stated. On the unusual occasion when the Lord went to the east side of the Sea of Galilee, the Scriptures indicate He came only to the borders of Decapolis, not into the heart of the Gentile area. The people He ministered to there were Jews in the predominantly Jewish area of the Tetrarchy of Phillip north of the boundary with Decapolis.

The location of the feeding of the 4,000 was probably somewhat south of the location of the earlier feeding of the 5,000. Both were in the Tetrarchy of Phillip near the Sea of Galilee and were miracles designed to show Israel that Jesus, the Messiah, was able to provide food miraculously for His people, much as Moses, by the power of God, was able to provide miraculous manna for the nation in the wilderness. They fit well into the Messianic program of our Lord in His presentation of the Kingdom to Israel. The concept of the Lord having a broad ministry among Gentiles could not be accomplished until His death and resurrection, and the beginning of the Church Age in the Book of Acts. When this extension of outreach beyond Israel did occur, the apostles were surprised, and had to be educated through miracles and Scriptural interpretation that the Lord had instituted a new program in the Church Age that included Gentiles.

Chapter 8
Correspondence
Concerning Textbooks

Our ministry, which airs a weekly Bible-teaching program with over a million viewers and issues monthly newsletters, receives a large volume of mail each day. Those of you who receive our monthly letters know that we often allow a generous amount of space to reprint some of this correspondence. Below are some excerpts from a small sampling of the correspondence we received regarding Gundry's errant textbook. I begin with the letter from Scott W. Bolinder, Senior Vice President and Publisher of Zondervan Publishers, who published Gundry's book:

> We regret that you have chosen to attack our author of some 28 years, Dr. Robert H. Gundry, and his book, *A Survey of the New Testament, 3rd edition.* We want to assure you that we would find it offensive and contrary to our editorial philosophy if any of our authors or books were found

to be anti-Semitic. But it is equally offensive when such a charge is leveled against one of our authors and books in a manner that is reckless, unjustified, arbitrary, and groundless.

As a result of your letters and TV program, a few letters and e-mail messages have been addressed to us where the writers have repeated your charges, though in most cases these people have clearly not read the book for themselves. Rather than just ignore these people, most of whom we believe to have a sincere concern for truth, we have chosen to respond by means of the letters enclosed.

As a Christian courtesy to you, we are sending you copies herewith. We would like to remind you that all correspondence is automatically protected by copyright law. You may reproduce these letters, or publicly read them, only if they are reproduced in their entirety without alteration.

Our desire would be that any such reproduction would be accompanied by a public apology to the author and Zondervan Publishing House.

If Zondervan received "a few letters and email messages" on this subject, then we received a hundred times as many. Our mailbox was choking with responses of which only a handful took exception to our battle. We will reprint a sampling of these letters below for the purpose of showing the clear perceptions of our audience to the theological issues. It sometimes seems as though the seminaries believe they can get away with anything and that the Christian public will be mystified by theology. That is not the case in this ministry and we have some 20 years experience with dynamic letters like those given below.

Zondervan's statements that our readers did not read the textbook for themselves is not really true. The letters below indicate a familiarity with the book on the part of those who comment. And besides, the appalling quality of Gundry's errors in the quotes we supplied in our Levitt Letter would certainly serve to indict the textbook, even if every other page of it were pristine and pure, which, of course, they were not.

Perhaps the reader of this book can gain from the observations in this variety of opinions. Since "Christians have all things in common" (Acts 2:45) and we share the mind of Christ, then we can learn from one another's views.

Where readers ask for information, it was provided by email or return letter in every case. Our office is very careful with requests, especially prayer requests, from our large readership.

And now, here's what some of our viewers have written:

Your television program regarding Robert H. Gundry's book, *A Survey of the New Testament*, was very enlightening. God said He would curse those who curse Israel. If the president and vice president of Criswell University failed to act, and in fact defended Gundry's book, they have, in effect, cursed Israel and will surely suffer the consequence God promised. They should voluntarily resign or be removed from their positions so the university does not also suffer from their error. I will do what I can to obtain that outcome. Thank you for alerting us regarding the above mentioned book.

The teacher at The Criswell College teaching Replacement Theology is Dr. Paul Wolfe. He seemed to be proud of the fact that he made his students angry and set about to "prove" to them that he is correct. It is a dangerous thing to blatantly teach falsely.

This is just to let you know that Robert H. Gundry's *A Survey of the New Testament; Third Edition* was a required textbook at The School of Lifelong Education (correspondence) at Oral Roberts University.

We are appalled at the blatant disregard for the Word. The attempt to control our youth by teaching false doctrine has now made it into our "Christian" environment. This practice is something that we are very familiar with. It was first used in our public education by the likes of Dewey and his ilk. They take small steps by introducing one or two incorrect or misleading things into textbooks (accepted as facts). Soon they have completely changed the direction of the nation's youth.

A young professor came and taught at our church about two weeks ago. He brought a lesson on Replacement Theology. He supposedly set out to prove that the church is now Israel. It was really quite pitiful. He teaches at The Criswell College which was also a surprise.

My daughter just graduated from Westmont College, where [Robert H.] Gundry was her Greek professor. We traveled to Santa Barbara for her graduation, and I was broadsided! On Friday night the Baccalaureate program included three students' reminiscent views of four years at Westmont. The first two were wonderful and encouraging. The third was given by... an Egyptian student graduating with a 4.0 in all four years of classes! According to my daughter, he had had no "campus life" because of his study schedule. Why he was honored with the platform was beyond most. His speech was not about campus life, the friends he had made, or how much he had grown in the L-rd, as were the first two. His tale was one of a trip he took to "the Middle East" while on Europe Semester. He met a woman who was awakened early one morning; she and her children were thrown out of their home and watched as the "oppressive Israeli soldiers" bulldozed the home of her dreams. A home that she had finally been able to afford on property her husband's family had owned since the Turkish occupation. Zola, I was enraged with righteous indignation. First, that this boy would tell half-truths and lies. You and I know that only the homes of convicted terrorists are destroyed, and the fact that the woman's husband was not evident validates this.

(A note from Zola: *You're probably right, but know that Israel also occasionally destroys homes built without proper permits on land that has been planned for other purposes. Palestinians tend to build houses in places that defy the Israeli administration of the land and sometimes only the bulldozer is effective. Your overall point that this odious subject was included in a graduation program shows the anti-Israel position of Westmont College.*)

✡   ✡   ✡   ✡   ✡   ✡   ✡

Battles with Seminaries: Defending Israel

Would you believe that just this summer one of our church members (Evangelical Free Church) presented a Sunday School class on the differences of the feeding of the 5,000 and the 4,000 and said the 4,000 were Gentiles?

This summer my daughter (in-law)...was given curriculum to use in a Vacation Bible School class. As she was telling me about it, she mentioned that the 4,000 fed by Jesus were Gentiles. That sent me right to my Bible, as I'd never heard that before. I couldn't find anywhere that was stated. Though I've studied the Bible for 22 years, taken Bible college courses and taught Bible studies on occasion, I'm certainly no expert. I was about to chalk up the 4,000 "Gentiles" to my ignorance, when your letter came. I took it to [my daughter-in-law], and she was amazed. She said there was no way she would teach that the 4,000 were Gentiles after reading what you said and what Thomas S. McCall wrote.

I know that the Bible says many will turn from His ways in the last days, but I am amazed that so many from so-called evangelical institutions and churches have strayed from God's Word.

I agree with you completely that this book is heresy, but since I know other things about Biola and Westmont that are very troubling, I'm not surprised by very much of anything they do.

Correspondence Concerning Textbooks

I am enclosing some letters that I have written to our own church's college and seminary, and one I wrote to Criswell. Bethel [College] does not teach any prophecy to speak of. I have been battling their seminary graduates for years. They teach that the Tribulation has always been on earth, etc. I could go on and on. I tell you one thing, Bethel does not get a dime of money or support from me. I marvel that the Lord lets it go on. Judgment day will come for these professors who have taught untruths about God's Word and His promises to the Jewish people and Israel. I am sure the Lord is not pleased.

You mentioned the use of the textbook A Survey of the New Testament, by Robert H. Gundry. I agree with your opinion that it is anti-Israel. I called D.B.U. [Dallas Baptist University] and asked who used it to teach from, and I was told Professor Tabares.

I am a prospective student seeking admission for this fall semester. The receipt of your letter today confirmed the reservations I had about this college, and yet I desire to go to a good Baptist college desperately. Can you please rec-ommend a "Jewish-friendly" school here in the U.S.?

Continue attacking Gundry's book! We are amazed to learn

127

(from you) [that] he was tossed out of the very seminary that now uses his book. Hypocritical! Thank God, your son is alert to anti-Semitic literature. God bless him and you for speaking out.

Through your television program, I learned that subject text is being used at Dallas Baptist University. That University is scheduled to inherit my estate.

I notified the Development Department of DBU that my estate will not come to DBU if subject text is retained, especially as required reading.

Parents trust professors to present truthful material to the young minds of their children and grandchildren they send there, often at considerable financial sacrifice. The professors who are responsible for this text's being in the lineup should have had at least a first clue by the picture of the Turk on a donkey. The other more subtle parts of the book that bruise my sensibilities should not be subtle in the minds of these professors who have served in their capacities for decades.

If this were a text in some other discipline, the impact would soon be felt in application; however, religion is the backbone of DBU and the department of highest need for discernment. It is not enough to say that everyone can have his own opinion. The text is blatantly in error throughout.

It saddens my heart that Gundry would write such a text, that the professionals at DBU whom parents trust to teach and guide have betrayed that trust—and evidently unwittingly for some reason (I can only guess)—and that it falls to us who care for the institution and the faculty who have sacrificed over the years to bring DBU where it is today, to bring pressure at the risk of antagonizing those we care for. Is this not true throughout the Word for those who will not participate in or condone the watering down of the Word that seems to be vogue today?

I have been reading your newsletter lately about the Replacement Theology in our seminaries. I, like you, am appalled at the lack of diligence to guard the truth. It appears to me that real God-given truth is becoming a scarce commodity in our teaching institutions. If we graduate leaders of the church with such notions, then I feel that God will have no other choice than to cause a real grass-roots upheaval. We non-seminary trained Bible theologians can easily see through this deception.

However, this fact doesn't change anything. Gentiles are not God's chosen people. They never were, and they never will be. God chose Abraham. We, as Gentiles, must be secure in our position in Christ, and be happy as our Jewish brothers and sisters find the fulfillment of their heritage. We Gentiles are adopted, but no less heirs. Zola, keep up the pressure. There has always been something special about Jews who love Jesus. I stand with you, and pray that all believers study the Bible instead of just accepting what the preachers have to say on any matter. May Truth prevail!

Battles with Seminaries: Defending Israel

Just recently, I spoke to a "Christian" woman who was obviously challenged in her theology when I stated that Jesus is a Jew. I kindly offered her Biblical proof of this, which she rejected or rationalized.

My son is a freshman at Taylor University in Upland, Indiana. I learned from your newsletter that Taylor used the Gundry text, and so I sent a letter of concern to the president. Yesterday I received a call from the professor who uses the text. He wasn't sure what the term Replacement Theology and "gentilizing" the gospels meant which I find interesting in itself. But nonetheless, I explained Replacement Theology. In our conversation he was not defensive but more curious and asked if I had suggestions for another text. Of course I drew a blank and feel I missed an opportunity. Can you help me in this matter?

This pertains to your letter about A Survey of the New Testament. We asked a Dr. Overstreet of Northwest Baptist Seminary in Tacoma, WA, if they were using this Gundry's book in their classes and he said, "Yes, we do."

I am so glad to see you renouncing certain books being used in the seminaries. Too many of these so-called halls of higher learning are producing Christians who have no clue that Christ was actually a Jew, Christians who have no love for their brothers and sisters in Christ (if they are of a denomination other than their own), much less a desire to see Israel restored to her original nobility!

I commented in my introduction to this letter section that we received very few negative comments about our textbook project, but now I share with you a letter from a disgruntled reader who seems to place a higher authority upon men and institutions rather than upon God:

> My spirit is deeply troubled at the conduct of this so-called Christian organization. You have directly attacked respected Christian leaders in a manner that lacks tact and biblical honor.
>
> I could begin to debate all of your issues as many have ventured to do before me. However, I feel that would be a waste of time on both our parts. I am primarily concerned about your conduct in light of the faith you claim to have.
>
> Was it not the Christ who explained that a tree would be judged by its fruit? You have attacked several major Christian schools and organizations which have been effective in Kingdom work for years on end.
>
> Indeed, there will be problems and concern in anyplace as long as sin exists in the world. The concerns you raise regarding doctrine, administrators, faculty, and standards have been recognized and dealt with as these leaders see fit. Who are you to bring into question these leaders' integrity? I warn you as a brother in the faith, when you slander

or question Christian authority, the Scripture tells us that you will be judged at a higher level.

It saddens me to think that there are people like your Thomas McCall who are so bitter that they find it behooves them to question the church body and work against it for personal satisfaction. Know well that the work you are trying to do is contrary to the work of the Holy Spirit. I challenge you to come before God and examine these means of communication and the thoughts that you are carelessly throwing out into the public arena.

May God have mercy on you!

Here was my written response:

I'm honestly a bit surprised by the tone of your letter. Please know that God must have constant mercy on this small ministry, or else we would never survive. During times when we take up difficult issues in the ministry of rebuke, I am especially sensitive to our letters and our support. Some remonstrate with us, as you have. Some simply get off our mailing list immediately. But the vast majority, aware of our Christ-like motives for what we do, pray for us and support us in good measure.

To answer your specific points, we certainly agree that "several major Christian schools and organizations" have been "effective...for years on end," but they have not accomplished that without constructive criticism. Rather than your conception that the administrations, faculty, etc., know the problems and have recognized and "dealt with them," problems are more likely swept under the rug.

And I'm not sure what you meant by "Christian authority." There are no authorities under the cross; we are all equal in Christ. The people who read the letters coming to our ministry are as important to the Lord as the presidents of the major seminaries (and much more straightforward and learned in the faith, I have found). And who am I to "bring into question these leaders' integrity?" Well, I'm a bondservant of Christ, like you, and I study the Scriptures. And I love Israel and support it, and I want correct doctrine at our seminaries.

Believe me when I tell you that Tom McCall and I find little personal satisfaction in doing the difficult work of correcting doctrinal errors. Our standards were set by the Lord, and by Peter and Paul and the other apostles who corrected doctrinal errors on a constant basis.

And finally, the public arena is the place to air these grievances, because the seminaries belong to the public, and it is the public which donates to them, pays for them and sends their children to them, trusting that the students will emerge with accurate Bible knowledge. I don't think that I will be judged at a higher level than you or anyone else will be, but I trust that I am accomplishing what the Lord has inspired me to do, and that He will be pleased with what I have done when I see Him in heaven.

As for judging a tree by its fruit, you may examine the works of this ministry anytime. We are candid and aboveboard in all we are doing, and our financial statements are yours for the asking. We do not have pressured workers or secret meetings or a powerful administration intimidating a frightened staff, like some organizations we deal with. In fact, you're welcome in our offices anytime, and I think you will be greeted by the warmth and love of true Christian fellowship. And those are, as best as I can explain them, our fruits.

Battles with Seminaries: Defending Israel

To those of you who have received defamatory letters about me from The Criswell College, I can only say that the issue is about the Gundry book and that is all. As I have said previously, I don't believe that the tactic of attacking the messenger has any place in Christian discourse.

Chapter 9
Conclusion

Inaccurate Christian books abound because unscriptural writers abound. The danger, however, occurs when these books, presumably about Scripture, wind up in the hands of students training to be pastors, missionaries, and seminary professors. It is particularly dangerous when the teacher using the errant textbooks is well-liked. We often subscribe carte blanche to the views of those in whom we put the most trust. How many pastors are wrongly teaching their congregations these days with references to Gundry's views on Israel and the New Testament?

We are happy that some schools looked seriously at the problem book and pulled it from their curriculum. Many more, however, refused to even acknowledge that a problem exists! We provide contact information at the end of the book for you to be informed about our variety of responses from seminaries.

My son, Aaron, writes a fitting conclusion to this battle as it unfolded at The Criswell College.

✿ ✿ ✿ ✿ ✿ ✿ ✿

Battles with Seminaries: Defending Israel

My Latest Adventure at The Criswell College **◆**

I arranged to sit in on a single class in the New Testament Survey course at The Criswell College, wondering if they were still using the Gundry textbook. When I arrived and introduced myself to Dr. [Roy] Metts, the instructor of the course, he suddenly began to look ill at ease. He said his 7:45 a.m. class had four students, only one of whom would be present today, and asked if I would like to wait for his 9:30 a.m. class. The 9:30 class is a Greek exegetical Master's Degree course, which he said covers material similar to the survey course I had requested. He said I was welcome to attend that one. I asked what time it was over. With a gracious tone, he said I could leave whenever I liked (I supposed now was preferable to him).

Because the Master's Degree course is far more advanced than what I was looking for, and because I was specifically interested in the New Testament survey courses, I asked if the survey class would continue to meet as scheduled, every Wednesday. He then told me that the class I had been signed up to attend was this Greek exegetical one. Then Mark Taplette, with whom I had arranged the class visitation, showed up and introduced himself, also seeming a little nervous. He, too, tried to convince me to attend the upper-level class, but Dr. Metts explained I wanted the NT survey course—the one where the Gundry book was involved. Mr. Taplette then took me down the hall to check the posted class schedules. He looked for a long time at them. Then he started to point at one, but stopped and said

---

◆ Originally featured in our April 1999 *Levitt Letter*.

to himself, "Oh, that's Dr. Wolfe's class." (Dr. Paul Wolfe is a Replacement Theologian who had offended me a year before. He was evidently still using the Gundry book in his class.) He found me five other class times for the NT survey course, which I wrote down. Then I asked him why he had arranged for me to attend the wrong course—the Master's Greek class instead of the survey course I had requested in writing (also wondering why he did not tell me of this switch when he called me to say I had permission to attend). He replied that there wasn't a survey course in the morning (for I had requested the morning) and that this Master's Degree course covered some of the same material.

Exasperated, I went into the bookstore and asked the clerk if there was a list of the required books for each course in the fall semester. She replied that the list is not out this early. I then asked if there was a list for the current semester, so that I could at least get an idea of the books required for a New Testament Survey course. She responded, "You mean the Gundry book?" When I answered yes, she told me that Dr. Metts always uses one certain book. Since I hadn't mentioned Dr. Metts, she seemed to have heard about my trying to sit in on the class. She gave me her book list, which indicated that two NT survey courses use the Gundry book as a required text (which is one more than in the previous semester, as reported to us by Dr. Lamar Cooper). One course is taught by Dr. William Johnston, a previous NT survey professor of mine, and the other by Metts himself. Thus, my former teacher is still using the book, and Dr. Metts, my erstwhile "host," as well.

So, far from de-emphasizing the book, the college has doubled its use, as far as I could tell. In reality, I think it would take the FBI to penetrate their system and get the facts.

Battles with Seminaries: Defending Israel

Over the course of this battle about Bible school textbooks, we have received conflicting letters from teachers and administration officials alike. The tactics used to dissuade this ministry from publicizing their use of blatantly unbiblical textbooks have at times reverted, unfortunately, to personal attacks against myself and the others who are engaged in this ministry of confrontation.

What we have discovered in contacting any number of these institutions is that one must be cautious of well-worn policy statements and sugar-coated assurances from "highly-respected" administrators and professors. While it is difficult at any given time to know for certain which schools are using Gundry's or any other flawed textbook, I would urge you to contact any school directly and thoroughly research 1) the doctrinal statements which their faculty must sign, and 2) the textbooks that are required reading in Bible teaching courses, in particular. Ask God to give you wisdom and discernment before you or your children attend any of these schools.

Part Three

Battle over Dispensationalism

Chapter 10
Progressive Dispensationalism

God wrote the Bible for everyone to know and understand. The great result of the Reformation was the breaking of chains that held the Bible prisoner in the priests' language and translating it into the common language of men. The use of the Koine Greek language in the New Testament, as opposed to classical Greek, illustrates, I believe, the fact that God did not intend only the highly educated to read and understand His Word. Koine was a "marketplace" Greek used by the average citizen at that time. It would be inaccurate to say that God expects us to do "mental gymnastics" in order to understand His will revealed in His Word. And this is the beauty of dispensationalism.

Normative dispensationalism has at its very root a sensible approach to Scripture. God used different ways of dealing with men at different times in man's history. Thus, in large terms, He utilized law in Old Testament times and grace in New Testament times. He conducted different spiritual economies or *dispensations* according to man's behavior and what man needed in any given period. Dispensationalism takes into account the literal-historical-grammatical manner of understanding the Bible; it's literally taking God at His Word. It sounds oversimplified, but it is really just a common sense way of reading and understanding the Bible. So, when God talks about Israel, we understand Him to mean *Israel*. When He speaks of the Church, He means the *Church*, not Israel. This is not to say that God is, or that dispensationalists are inflexible literalists when interpreting the Bible. We recognize that God allowed His Word to be written through the creative pens of men, who recorded Scripture not simply as historical narrative, but also in grammatical forms such as poetry, proverbs, songs, symbolism, figures of speech, etc. Again, it's a common-sense approach to reading and interpreting Scripture.

Unfortunately, once this literal method of understanding the Bible is degraded, once a theologian (or any of us for that matter) begins to re-interpret God's Word using two different hermeneutics, one literal and one allegorical, then the result is a confusing, muddled understanding of what God is saying. And that is just where we find ourselves today with the new teaching called *Progressive Dispensationalism* or PD, as we will refer to it.

This teaching, more than the previous two "battles" in which we were engaged, is perhaps the most far-reaching in its effect upon seminaries, their faculties, and, most importantly, their graduates. Infiltrating the top conservative, evangelical seminaries in this country, PD's fundamental flaw—minimizing the distinction between the Church and Israel—could result in the downfall of dispensational teaching, particularly with regard to the prophecies regarding and, therefore, the attitudes toward God's present and future work in the nation Israel and His Chosen People, the Jews.

It will be no surprise to you that once again the responses we have received from these institutions have been less than welcoming. Despite doctrinal statements staring them in the face, the leaders of these schools have chosen to "tolerate" PD rather than deal with it in its infancy. As we will discuss later, the implications are far-reaching—even into your own Sunday school classrooms! And this is our primary concern.

What are you and your children learning about Scripture, about what God has to say concerning the Rapture of the Church, concerning the Tribulation and Second Coming of Messiah, concerning Christ reigning on David's throne for 1,000 years in Israel? And if we are to receive little or no teaching about Israel's future in God's plan, what becomes of our attitude toward the nation of Israel today? Is it simply a sinful work of man's hands, or is the re-establishment of the nation a miraculous work of God as the beginning of prophetic fulfillment?

These questions must be dealt with in our seminaries, but increasingly are not. In the following pages, you will discover why.

The following articles, the first of which appeared in our February 2000 *Levitt Letter*, introduce this last and most arduous battle in which we were engaged.

✡   ✡   ✡   ✡   ✡   ✡   ✡

The Awful Untruth

We have fought a lengthy battle on the field of dispensationalism. Our objective was to confront the teaching called Progressive Dispensationalism, a doctrine we discovered back at Dallas Seminary, which has now infected Moody Bible Institute, Talbot Seminary, Biola College, Dallas Baptist University and any number of other formerly fine, trustworthy Bible teaching institutions. Some of the formerly dispensational seminaries, teaching the very logical system of spiritual economies given in the Bible, have departed into this strange teaching which takes a negative view of modern Israel, and that is our chief objection. Like Amillennialism, a doctrine which holds that there will be no future Kingdom on earth, Progressive Dispensationalism considers modern Israel to be the work of man and not of God. It rejects the concept of God's covenant with an unsaved Israel such as we have today. Despite the teachings of the "dry bones" vision [Ezek. 37] and any number of other passages, Progressive Dispensationalists demand a believing Israel before they will accept it as a nation regathered by divine miracle.

In fact, these theologians have adopted the politically correct view that Israel is oppressing the Palestinians. They are apparently convinced by the media's negative reports despite the plain evidence of the eyes of any pilgrim who goes to the land.

The Progressive Dispensationalist teachers ignore the resurgence of the Messianic movement in Israel and even the heartening spread of faith in Yeshua (Jesus) among the Jews in this country. They seem not to understand how the situation in modern Israel will lead to the Tribulation and the Millennium, which is very clear even to Sunday school teachers everywhere. They seem embarrassed about the idea of Israel becoming the head of the nations, and they think that an emphasis on Israel somehow diminishes the church.

They seem to de-emphasize the study of eschatology—or prophecy—entirely. There has been a decline of prophecy conferences nationwide and little teaching of Revelation going on these days in the pulpits or classrooms. There is, in particular, a reduced teaching of the Pre-Tribulation Rapture which is arguably the doctrine of prime importance to the church today. The fact that the Lord can come at any moment ought to have a profound influence on every Christian!

☆   ☆   ☆   ☆   ☆   ☆   ☆

The Doctrine of Progressive Dispensationalism ✦

by Todd Baker, ThM

Today there is a growing movement within dispensational theology that is gaining influence among some leading dispensational seminaries and churches across the land. It is called "Progressive Dispensationalism." Traditional dispensationalism has always maintained a clear distinction between Israel and the Church, and that the Messianic Kingdom, of which the Davidic Covenant (2 Sam. 7:8-16; Ps. 89) is a main feature, still is a future *earthly* event that will occur when Christ returns to Jerusalem to reign over the earth for 1,000 years (Rev. 19:11 - 20:1-6).

However, proponents of Progressive Dispensationalism have changed some of this with their interpretation of Acts 2 (particularly verses 30-36). They teach from Acts 2:30 that the throne of God in heaven where Jesus now sits is the throne of David. Hence, Jesus is currently reigning from David's throne in heaven,

---

✦ When we started our battle against Progressive Dispensationalism, we received a number of letters asking for a clear definition of it. I asked Todd Baker, one of our ministry theologians, to prepare the following explanation of this doctrine. Todd's article originally appeared in our May 2000 *Levitt Letter*.

and the Messianic Kingdom is now inaugurated and is beginning to be fulfilled! What was once clearly a future event is now, somehow, a present reality. This is a disturbing departure from a normal literal understanding of Bible prophecy that views the throne of David as an *earthly throne* Christ will sit on and reign from Jerusalem when He returns (Isa. 2:1-5; Ezek. 43:1-7).

To believe this is now being "progressively" fulfilled blurs the distinction between Israel and the Church and minimizes the prophetic importance and position of modern-day Israel. The context of Acts 2 does not teach that Jesus is now reigning on the throne of David. Rather, the main point of Peter's sermon is that God has demonstrated the man Jesus, who was crucified by the Jewish leaders, to be "both Lord and Christ" by the following three events in Acts 2: (1) by the resurrection v. 31; (2) by the exaltation at God's right hand v. 33, and (3) by sending the Holy Spirit of promise v. 33. The gist of Acts 2:30-36 is that Christ's resurrection and exaltation at the right hand of God on the heavenly throne guarantees His future reign on the earthly Davidic throne as David's Lord and greater descendant.

Nowhere in Acts or, for that matter, in the entire Bible does one find the earthly throne of David and the heavenly throne of God explicitly identified as ever being the same. They are always *distinct* and *different* in Scripture. In the book of Acts, it is even more obvious and evident that Christ is not presently reigning on the throne as David, as Progressive Dispensationalism claims. Luke opens Acts with Christ's post-resurrection ministry to the disciples for forty days. During that time, Jesus spoke to them "of things pertaining to the *Kingdom of God*" (Acts 1:3). Surely, in all that time, if Jesus were to shortly reign on the throne of David in heaven, He would have plainly told them of this important change and transference of David's throne from earth to heaven when they asked Him, "Lord, are you at this time going to restore the Kingdom to Israel?" (Acts 1:6). Christ did not reply, "You are mistaken about this Jewish misconception of an earthly throne and Kingdom in Israel. The throne of David has been transferred to the throne of God in heaven where I will ascend and shortly reign from."

Instead, Jesus told the disciples that God the Father has appointed the time and season in the future when the Davidic Kingdom will be established in Israel (Acts 1:7). In the meantime, they were to go out and preach the Gospel in all the world, starting in Jerusalem (Acts 1:8). The Davidic rule and Kingdom did not begin when the Lord ascended to heaven, or He would have obviously told them so when questioned about the time and season for the establishment of the Kingdom in Israel. If Jesus is currently reigning on David's throne in heaven, then Acts 15:16-18 contradicts this novel idea of Progressive Dispensationalism. The passage in Acts 15 deals with the issue of Gentile salvation and whether or not Gentiles must be circumcised and observe the Mosaic law to become Christians. James answers for the group at the Jerusalem Council by saying the calling-out of Gentile believers is in keeping with the *future* promise of a *Davidic Kingdom* in *Israel*. Once the present age ends after the taking out of a Gentile body of believers "for His name" (a distinct characteristic and divine work of the present age), Christ will return to *rebuild* and *restore "the tabernacle of David."* The phrase "Tabernacle of David" is a descriptive synonym of the Davidic throne and earthly Kingdom that has long been in ruins (Acts 15:16). It still remains this way during the present age and awaits the final restoration at the return of Christ to earth. If Christ was reigning on the throne of David in heaven at this time, why then did James say the Davidic monarchy was still in ruins? The only reasonable and clear answer is that Jesus has yet to

147

return to earth to repair and rebuild it when He comes to reign on an earthly throne of David in Jerusalem, not heaven.

Clearly, in the book of Acts, the Jewish disciples, along with the Jewish Church of Jerusalem, were looking forward to a future earthly literal Davidic Messianic Kingdom in Israel to be ruled over by the Messiah Jesus. It was not spiritualized and transferred to heaven where Christ presently is, contrary to the belief of Progressive Dispensationalism. Carried to its logical conclusion, Progressive Dispensationalism could lead to saying the Church is Israel, followed by a denial of the Jewish people's status as God's Chosen People and the vital role Israel will play in the future Davidic Kingdom to come. Christ is King over the created universe and His Church. He will be an earthly King over a redeemed Israel as their Davidic ruler on David's earthly throne when He returns to earth. Therefore, Christ's rule from the throne of David totally awaits a future fulfillment currently not realized now.

Chapter 11
Correspondence with Seminary Presidents

As is often the case in large organizations, getting through to the decision maker can be tough. This is especially true with the presidents of our major seminaries and Bible schools. Yes, they're quite busy, not only (or perhaps mostly) with the day-to-day operations of the school, but also with speaking engagements, conferences, interviews, pastoral ministries, etc. But when a problem comes to the surface that has the potential to negatively affect graduates and, subsequently, local churches, one might think that the president would have time to respond. Much of the time we have found this not to be so.

In our current confrontation of the erroneous doctrine of Progressive Dispensationalism, these leaders have often relegated such tasks to administrative assistants, from whom we received a number of letters either directly or through our viewers. I debated whether to print them for you to read, but I found that they were all singing the same tune, almost word for word.

Battles with Seminaries: Defending Israel

No doubt, each of these assistants had been given guidelines and parameters for their correspondence with our ministry. So much so, it seems, that they also repeated the same criticisms about me, using words like "misinformed" and "alarmist," among others.

Following are letters from four seminary presidents concerning the issue of Progressive Dispensationalism.

Dr. Charles R. Swindoll
President, Dallas Theological Seminary
Dallas, Texas

Although Charles Swindoll has never fully engaged us in our theological concerns about PD taught at Dallas Seminary, he did finally answer us personally. It should be noted that Dr. Swindoll is on his way out of DTS leadership in order to focus his efforts on his new church in Frisco, Texas. In addition, he maintains daily radio broadcasts with his organization, Insight for Living. It is easy to see that he would rather not enter the fray when someone else, presumably Dr. Mark Bailey, will be taking over leadership in a few month's time. Although Dr. Swindoll may not personally agree with PD, he chooses to stay out of the line of fire in this particular battle, leaving the bulk of responses to underlings in the administration. Here's Swindoll's letter to me:

> One of our faculty members recently shared with me the June 2000 issue of your publication in which you are critical of our school. I'm concerned that you don't have the full picture, and that you are jumping to wrong conclusions.

Correspondence with Seminary Presidents

Your assistant, Dr. McCall, needs to know that all of us on the seminary faculty sign our doctrinal statement annually. Furthermore, our faculty members *are* publishing books and articles. He also needs to be aware that even though a few faculty members may teach Progressive Dispensationalism, that position does not represent a drift in our commitment to premillennialism, nor does it mean that at Dallas Seminary "prophecy is neglected," or that the belief in the rapture has begun "to wane."

I can assure you that we still teach and write on prophecy and certainly that we still believe, teach, and write on the rapture. Our long-standing commitment to dispensational theology and especially our historic position on pretribulational premillennialism remain firmly in place. In fact, we are currently publishing four articles on the rapture in four issues of our *Bibliotheca Sacra* Journal.

Here are some recent books from our faculty for your review:

The New Testament Explorer
Dr. Mark Bailey and Dr. Tom Constable

A Case for Premillennialism
Dr. Donald K. Campbell

The Rise of Babylon
Dr. Charles H. Dyer

World News and Bible Prophecy
Dr. Charles H. Dyer
Three Central Issues in Contemporary Dispensationalism

Dr. Darrell Bock, Dr. Elliot Johnson,
Dr. Stanley Touissaint and Dr. Lanier Burns

Hope Again
Dr. Charles Swindoll

Every Prophecy of the Bible
Dr. John F. Walvoord

End Times
Dr. John F. Walvoord

Vital Prophetic Issues
Dr. Roy B. Zuck

I hope this sets the record straight regarding the seminary's theological convictions and that publications *continue* to come from Dallas Seminary concerning prophecy and the rapture of the church.

Dr. McCall made these astute observations about Dr. Swindoll's letter in our September 2000 *Levitt Letter*:

The 10 books he lists were published during the last ten years by some 11 current and former faculty members. The problem is that nine of the authors are in what must be considered the old guard of the seminary, who have not changed doctrinally, and only two could be considered in the new crop of professors. That is precisely the problem we were pointing out, that the most of the new professors, some of whom have adopted the aberrant view of Progressive Dispensationalism and other problematical doctrines, were not publishing any works which could be evaluated. In one sense, I

Correspondence with Seminary Presidents

am glad that they are not publishing their views, but on the other hand, it makes it difficult to evaluate concepts that are not published, but are only taught in the cloistered halls of the classrooms.

Furthermore, Dr. Swindoll responded to one of our faithful readers who wrote to him, stating his concern that the seminary was teaching doctrines that produced a negative attitude toward modern Israel, and Dr. Swindoll laid down the following challenge:

> Many of our theological statesmen continue to teach here. This prestigious list includes: Dr. John F. Walvoord, Dr. J. Dwight Pentecost, Dr. Robert P. Lightner, Dr. Howard G. Hendricks, and Dr. Stanley D. Toussaint. This is not a list for a publicity brochure...each of these men is *active in the classrooms.*
>
> Candidly, every one of our professors signs our doctrinal statement when they renew their annual contract. All have signed it for this new academic year. *If you know of a teacher here who is teaching outside of that document, please name the professor and send it to my attention.* I have included our doctrinal statement for your convenience. [Emphasis ours]

It is with great sadness that I raise pen in hand to respond to the challenge presented by the president of my alma mater Dallas Theological Seminary, Dr. Charles Swindoll. Let us first make clear that we have always appreciated the ministry of Dr. Swindoll, especially on his regular radio program, in which his expository sermons in his church are broadcast widely throughout North America. Neverthe-

153

less, several years ago he became president of DTS, and has thus presided over the gradual shift of the seminary into the erroneous doctrine, which the adherents call Progressive Dispensationalism.

In his letter to us, Dr. Swindoll admits that a few of the professors at DTS are teaching Progressive Dispensationalism, but that he thinks this does not violate the doctrinal statement. We are aware of at least *five* of the newer professors who are openly teaching Progressive Dispensationalism at DTS. Furthermore, we have shown repeatedly in this newsletter that Progressive Dispensationalism is in error, and that it contradicts at least one of the articles of the doctrinal statement of the seminary, the one forbidding any confusion in the dispensations of Law, Grace and the Millennium.

Nevertheless, Dr. Swindoll does not think that Progressive Dispensationalism violates the doctrinal statement or the Scriptures. We vehemently believe it does. Who is right? We appeal to one of the "theological statesmen" at DTS whom Dr. Swindoll mentions above, Dr. Robert P. Lightner, who writes the following statement of concern in an article in *The Conservative Theological Journal*, Vol. 4, No. 11, March 2000, entitled "Progressive Dispensationalism" (emphasis added):

> I certainly want to make it clear that I don't think anybody at Dallas Seminary has an evil agenda. I don't believe anyone is trying to undermine and destroy the seminary. Neither has anybody there, as far as I know, in his own public statements and proclamations, denied any of the essentials of the faith.

What concerns me, *and a host of others*, are some of the things that have been *tolerated*, and in fact *promoted* by some faculty members. *We are fearful of the future.* We are afraid of the long, *slippery slope* and of what will happen. We have that fear, not just out of emotionalism, but out of a reflection on history. *This is exactly what happened in other organizations and institutions.* There are no sudden landslides in the Christian community, even in a Christian's life. Instead, there is always *a gradual trickling and slipping away of the foundation*, picking at the foundation *until eventually there is nothing worthwhile left. This is our concern.*

One of the cardinal truths of the Scripture emphasized by mainstream dispensationalists is that the Church Age is a previously unrevealed *parenthesis* the Lord inserted into the previously revealed prophetic program. Later in this same excellent article, Dr. Lightner rebuts the view of the Progressive Dispensationalists, who object to this standard dispensational teaching:

[The Progressive Dispensationalists teach that] the Church is not a *parenthesis* or *intercalation* in God's program. They resent that terminology. I think that's Ironside's or Scofield's terminology, parenthesis; Chafer's is intercalation. I think both are good terms, but progressives don't like them at all. The Dallas Theological Seminary's doctrinal statement is *crystal clear* in stating that there are three absolutely indispensable critical dispensations. It doesn't argue for seven. It says there are *three* musts; three indispensable ones, law, grace or Church, and Kingdom, and it says the three must *never* be intermingled. They remain totally distinct. Do the progressives keep the Church and the Kingdom totally distinct? I should say not; they combine the two. *That's a flagrant violation of the DTS Doctrinal Statement.* (Emphasis added)

Thus we see that one of the theological statesmen of the current professors of Dallas Theological Seminary reports with much sorrow and anguish of soul that the professors at the seminary who are teaching Progressive Dispensationalism are in *flagrant violation* of the DTS Doctrinal Statement, and that this is being *tolerated* by the administration.

Our critics may say, so what? Isn't this just theological nitpicking? What concerns us most are the results of this aberrant teaching, especially as it relates to the Christian attitude toward modern Israel. The Progressive Dispensational teaching that the modern nation of Israel has no relation to the fulfillment of Bible prophecy is blinding the eyes of many evangelical Christians to what the Lord is doing *now* in preparation for the Second Coming of Christ. Their erosion of the Scriptural teaching of the distinctiveness of God's program for the Church from God's program for Israel is dulling the anticipation of the blessed hope, the Rapture. These are serious negative results stemming from bad theological teaching. Pray that these schools will return to the anchor of the unadulterated Word of God.

I've had great respect for Dr. Swindoll for many years, but I'm disappointed in his status quo answer. Most of those he lists as publishing books on prophecy and dispensationalism are from the "old guard" of the seminary who wouldn't think of deviating from normative dispensationalism and whose books were written some time ago.

Dr. John F. Walvoord
Chancellor, Dallas Theological Seminary
Dallas, Texas

Another former DTS president, now chancellor of DTS, is Dr. John Walvoord, who has been on our television program a number of times. He is a rare soldier for Christ. Still traveling and teaching, he nevertheless takes time to come to our small program. Over 80 years old, he showed up once on crutches.

He wrote to us concerning Dallas Seminary and Progressive Dispensationalism:

Recently, I listened to your telecast on Sunday, February 13, in which you made remarks along with Dr. McCall about Dallas Theological Seminary.

From my point of view, some of these remarks were not quite accurate, and I would like to submit what I believe to be the true situation.

As you noted, some teachers at Dallas Theological Seminary are advancing what they call Progressive Dispensationalism. This is an unfortunate word because dispensationalism has always been progressive, because beginning with the Garden of Eden, the moral code required of believers changes as additional revelation is given. The Book of Genesis records a series of dispensations, one following the other. In each case, some of the moral code of the preceding dispensation is incorporated in the new dispensation. Some requirements are canceled and other new requirements are added, and that continues as long as there is additional revelation from God. Dr. [Charles] Ryrie's analysis that the main point of Progressive Dispensationalism is that Christ is presently on the throne of David in heaven is true. A departure to amillennialism is not true.

In the Old Testament, the major dispensation was the Mosaic Law, which incorporated more than six hundred regulations covering almost every phase of human conduct, which was imposed on the nation Israel but never on the whole world. In the New Testament as John 1 records, grace and truth came by Jesus Christ; that is, in our present age we were in an age of grace where the Mosaic Law is no longer operative.

While some factors in the Mosaic Law are continued, others are canceled; for example, we do not go to Jerusalem several times a year and offer animal sacrifices. On the other hand, the Ten Commandments are continued in the sense that nine of them are repeated. The only one omitted is the fourth commandment dealing with the Sabbath, and Christians are not under the regulation to observe Saturday as the day of rest.

I personally disagree with so-called progressive dispensationalists, because they argue that because Christ is the appointed Son of David to rule over Israel, that His throne in heaven now is the throne of Israel, which I do not believe is true. A throne is not a chair, but a sphere of rule. This is illustrated in David himself, who was appointed king many years before he began to reign and assume the throne. The same is true of Christ. While He has all the authority and power over Israel, He is not exercising it at the present time. Even though they assert that He is ruling over Israel, the facts are that there is no support for this, and non-Christian Jews would be very much surprised if they were told they were under the rule of Christ. When the millennial kingdom comes, Christ will set up His throne in Jerusalem, and He will rule over Israel and over the whole world in an absolute sovereignty, and any who oppose Him will be punished. This is in contrast to our present day of grace where God permits many to rebel against Himself without immediate punishment.

I have talked to those who hold the progressive dispensational position and have asked them what their position is on other doctrines.

They have affirmed that they are pre-millennial; that is, they believe there will be a thousand-year reign of Christ on earth following His Second Coming. They are still pre-Tribulational in that they believe the Rapture will occur before the Tribulation. They distinguish between God's program prophetically for the Church and for Israel and recognize that, in the millennial kingdom, Israel will be restored as a nation and exalted and honored by Christ in a way that is not true today. They also affirm that, while they are holding to Progressive Dispensationalism, they are still dispensationalist and can sign the doctrinal statement of Dallas Seminary, because it really does not cover the issues involved in Progressive Dispensationalism. A teacher at the Seminary is judged entirely on the basis of how he relates to the doctrinal statement. All of the faculty and board members sign a statement each year affirming their faith in the doctrinal statement and their acceptance of it. There has been no change in our doctrinal statement. It is not true that the Seminary officially supports Progressive Dispensationalism, as none of the officials in the administration hold that position. In the light of these facts, it is not true that Dallas Seminary is leaning toward amillennialism, as this would involve taking non-literally the many passages on the millennial kingdom. It is not true that we are leaning to post-Tribulationism, because that would require spiritualization of the Tribulation, which we do not do.

The statement was made that we are silent on the subject of prophecy at the Seminary and do not hold prophecy conferences. This is not true. In the fall of 1998, the Seminary held a six-day prophecy conference in Prestonwood Baptist Church. The public was charged $50 for a registration fee and attended six nights. Two thousand people attended and paid the fee. The lectures given were later incorporated into a book and published by Word Publishing. The book entitled *The Road to Armageddon*, which has had a wide sale, is the official statement of the Seminary's position on prophecy, which is premillennial, pre-Tribulational and dispensational. After the conference at Prestonwood, there was a demand for additional instruction, and an all-day seminar was arranged at the Seminary. Dr. Stephen Bramer and I taught eight major subjects during the seminar and answered many questions from the floor. It was a reaffirmation of the Seminary's traditional position on eschatology.

The Seminary is also publishing a series of leadership books by the faculty, and sixteen of these will be in doctrinal areas. I was assigned to write on the subject of eschatology and wrote the book *End Times*, which is a detailed affirmation of the

Seminary's position on premillennialism, pre-Tribulationism and dispensationalism. It also has had a wide sale. Recently, I completed an eight-week Bible study at Northwest Bible Church in which *End Times* was used as a textbook, and I taught the section for each night in eight sections covering the entire book. About two hundred fifty people enrolled in this course and bought the book.

In addition to these declarations of our eschatological point of view, I am continually holding Bible conferences around the country in the area of prophecy and will be leaving shortly for a week in Florida. Recently, I spoke to four different groups in Dallas in one week on the subject of prophecy. It simply is not true that the Seminary is silent on the subject of prophecy or that we have changed our position.

It is always difficult for an institution to maintain doctrinal harmony, especially when it has more than sixty scholars who are independently studying the issues. It is our goal at Dallas Theological Seminary to require agreement on all major doctrine, but there is room for difference of opinion on minor things where even the best of scholars disagree.

It is possible for faculty members to depart from orthodoxy and teach contrary to the doctrinal statement. Through the years, we have had to dismiss some faculty for this purpose. There was one faculty member who was not clear on the doctrine of Biblical inerrancy, and his contract was not renewed. Another professor taught for years but then adopted the idea of limited atonement, that Christ died only for the elect, which is contrary to our doctrinal statement. He was not re-hired. In the first year of Dr. Campbell's presidency, three faculty members were dismissed. One of them was outspoken against dispensationalism, the other two had unrelated problems. In other words, when we find a faculty member seriously out of step with our doctrinal position, he is dismissed. But the judgment has to be based on difference with our doctrinal statement, not on things which our doctrinal statement does not cover.

If you have any evidence that any of our faculty disagrees with our doctrinal statement, we would appreciate it if you would give their name to me and the evidence, and I will see what I can do to find out the truth.

I have no desire for controversy with you and do not want to make this a public issue. I do not want this letter to be quoted unless you quote it in its entirety. But I think you should know that what you presented as the truth was not describing the actual situation.

Dr. Thomas S. McCall, ThD, a doctoral graduate of DTS, responds to Dr. Walvoord's letter:

We appreciate very much Dr. Walvoord's letter on the problem of Progressive Dispensationalism at Dallas Theological Seminary. He is one of the heroes of traditional Dispensationalism, is one of the greatest living prophecy teachers, and is currently serving as the Chancellor of the seminary. He has been on our television program on several occasions and is a true friend of the Gospel of Christ and of Israel. He has asked us to print his letter in its entirety, if we print any of it, and we have done so for your information and edification.

Dr. Walvoord explains with excellent clarity the Scriptural errors of Progressive Dispensationalism. He shows that the idea that Christ has assumed the throne of David and is ruling over Israel at the present time is obviously false and unscriptural. He indicates that he and Dr. Charles Ryrie are in agreement on the fact that this teaching of Progressive Dispensationalism is in error. The only question is how serious it is for professors in influential positions in seminary classrooms to be teaching this erroneous doctrine to future ministers of the churches. Dr. Walvoord states that, when professors have deviated seriously from the doctrinal statement of the seminary, they have left.

Does Progressive Dispensationalism conflict with the doctrinal statement of Dallas Seminary? What does a plain reading of the doctrinal statement (available on the DTS website) indicate? In Article 5, on Dispensationalism, it states:

> We believe that three of these dispensations or rules of life are the subject of extended revelation in the Scriptures, viz., the dispensation of the Mosaic law, the present dispensation of grace, and the future dispensation of the millennial kingdom. *We believe that these are distinct and are not to be intermingled or confused, as they are chronologically successive.* [Emphasis ours]

Do you think that the concept that an emphatically millennial event such as the assumption of Christ on the throne of David at the present time is a confusion or intermingling of the current dispensation of grace and the future millennium? It would be interesting to know what our readers think of this. Can a professor who teaches Progressive Dispensationalism honestly sign the above doctrinal statement without reservation? Most of our readers are not trained theologians, but many are astute at evaluating Biblical truth.

Battles with Seminaries: Defending Israel

✡ ✡ ✡ ✡ ✡ ✡

Dr. Joseph M. Stowell
President, Moody Bible Institute
Chicago, Illinois

To date, we have yet to receive a personal response from Dr. Joseph Stowell of Moody Bible Institute. But he did apparently take time to answer one of our viewers concerning the problem of PD. We include that letter here:

I appreciate your writing to share your concerns about an article in Zola Levitt's February newsletter. We remain fully grounded in the doctrines that we were founded on by D. L. Moody over 110 years ago.

I can assure you that we do not see Israel as a product of man's effort, and not one of our faculty members would believe that. In fact, we have one of the finest Jewish studies programs in the nation. Each member of our faculty is a staunch adherent to the distinction between Israel and the church and believe that God has a prophetically prescribed future in store for Israel. Each year, our faculty members and administrative team are required to agree with and sign our Doctrinal Statement (which remains the same as originally adopted in 1928 by our Board of Trustees), which holds to a pre-tribulation Rapture view and a literal millennial reign of Christ.

✡ ✡ ✡ ✡ ✡ ✡ ✡

Correspondence with Seminary Presidents

Dr. Mal Couch
President, Tyndale Theological Seminary
Fort Worth, Texas

And finally, a letter of an altogether different nature from a seminary president. Dr. Mal Couch, ThD, heads a fine dispensational school, Tyndale Theological Seminary, in Fort Worth, Texas, and wrote to us recently regarding the problems many seminaries are having holding onto their doctrinal purity:

> I want to congratulate you on your ongoing expose in regard to what is happening in Christian schools. The general Christian public is in the dark about the spiritual deterioration that is rapidly changing the face of our evangelical denominations and seminaries.
>
> I know that you have taken criticism from many who think all is well in our conservative circles. But you are right on. The unending conversation of "older" evangelical leaders, authors, and Bible school teachers is in regard to the gradual destruction of our theological institutions.
>
> Some questions you have been asked are, "To what school do I send my child if he or she wants a Christian-based education?" and "How can I tell if the school is shifting away from strong and solid Biblical instruction?" Unfortunately, these are tough questions because neither the teachers' pedigrees nor the doctrinal statement of the institution will indicate a major change in instruction and belief. *There is underway a very subtle and diabolical degrading of truth that certainly won't show up in any publicized material.*
>
> To try to help, here are some areas to inquire into in order to try to find out what is going on in a given church or seminary:

1. What is their attitude in regard to feminism in general, and women in leadership positions in particular, in regard to spiritual guidance in churches?
2. Are secular psychological principles being taught in the counseling department in the institution?
3. Is there a de-emphasis in Bible prophecy, in the classrooms, in the doctrinal statement, or in the pulpit-teaching ministry of the church?
4. Is the school moving toward more "how-to" courses and away from the strong teaching of the Biblical languages and doctrine?
5. Is the faculty moving toward Progressive Dispensationalism and away from traditional dispensational teaching?
6. What is the attitude toward the Jewish people and the nation of Israel?
7. When examining the direction a church is moving, see what is its attitude toward hard Christian rock music and being "seeker" friendly. Is there a feeling that the church or institution is emphasizing a certain elitism, bigness, and even secularism? In other words, is it focusing on everything but the teaching of the Word of God?
8. Finally, check the length and depth of the doctrinal statement of the church or institution. Does it cover specific Biblical answers to issues like: abortion, feminism, secularism, evolution, homosexuality, psychology, materialism? Does it contain strong statements about the inspiration and inerrancy of Scripture? Does it address doctrinal issues like the Rapture, Tribulation, and the Second Coming of Christ?

Thank you for mentioning Tyndale as one of the more solid schools still around. By God's grace, we are definitely going to hold the line. May God bless you as you stand firm and expose the errors rapidly growing in our circles.

In all of our correspondence with Bible schools and seminaries, none was more difficult than with Moody Bible Institute, whose tactics in responding to our concerns were unfortunate, to put it kindly. In the next two chapters, Dr. McCall addresses these concerns and Moody's reactions to our inquiries.

Chapter 12
"Dyer" Circumstances at Moody *

"It may be that he has jumped from the frying pan into the fire," said one of Dr. Charles Dyer's colleagues. He was speaking of Dr. Dyer's recent move from Dallas Seminary to Moody Bible Institute. There were high hopes in conservative theological circles about this transition. Dr. Dyer has excellent credentials as a conservative dispensational theologian who loves the Lord and teaches the truth about the First and Second Comings of Christ. During the early stages of the Gulf War, he wrote a significant prophetic book about Babylon. He gave evidence of having a firm grasp on the problems of Progressive Dispensationalism. Many thought that Dr. Dyer might be able

---

* In the course of our dealing with the various seminaries, our viewers wrote to the presidents of those schools and in some cases, assistants were detailed to answer the questions. Dr. Stowell of Moody Bible Institute handed a viewer letter to Dr. Charles Dyer for a response. Dr.Thomas McCall deals with Dyer's answer in this article that appeared in the October 2000 *Levitt Letter*.

to correct some of the doctrinal problems at Moody we have been chronicling that are symptomatic of many of our formerly strong dispensational schools.

Thus, Dr. Dyer moved from Dallas Seminary, which has several Progressive Dispensational teachers, to Moody, which has similar, and other, problems. It may, indeed, be that he has jumped from the frying pan into the fire. No sooner had Dr. Dyer arrived in Chicago than President Stowell received a letter from one of our faithful and concerned readers about the new doctrines being taught at Moody. Dr. Dyer was asked to respond to this letter, and our reader sent it to us for analysis so that our readers could be aware of the arguments involved. Dyer found himself in the unenviable position of defending those who teach a doctrinal position at variance with his own and the long-held views of Moody Bible Institute. The heart of his response is contained in the following paragraphs:

> All dispensationalists must distinguish between the reality of God's present rule (called "the mystery form of the kingdom" by Dr. Pentecost) and the fact of Christ's future reign on earth during the millennial Kingdom. Progressive Dispensationalists and Classic Dispensationalists differ in how they describe the nature of God's present rule from heaven. However, the crucial issue that decides whether individuals are still within the boundaries of dispensationalism is not how they define Christ's rule today, but where they stand on the reality of Christ's rule during the millennial Kingdom. And Moody Bible Institute requires its faculty to agree to the following doctrinal beliefs that are crucial to dispensationalism:

- **Pretribulational Rapture:** Christ will return preceding the Great Tribulation at which time He will receive into heaven dead and living believers who constitute His Church.
- **Literal Second Coming and Millennium:** The premillennial return of Christ at which time He will set up his thousand-year reign.
- **Distinction between Israel and the Church:** The Church of Jesus Christ is a distinct entity from Israel in the program of God. We further believe that the Universal Church consists of all who possess saving faith in the death, burial, and resurrection of Jesus Christ from Pentecost to the Rapture of the Church and who will represent every language, tribe and nation.

Some individuals imply that if a person is a Progressive Dispensationalist, he or she cannot hold to the three statements just made. I know from experience that this is simply not true. Having read and interacted with a number of theologians who call themselves "Progressive Dispensationalists," I have learned that they do not all hold to the same beliefs in these areas. Some see a clear distinction between Israel and the Church, believe in the pretribulational Rapture of the Church, hold to a literal millennial Kingdom when Christ will reign over the whole earth from Jerusalem, and affirm a future for the nation Israel based on God's promises to them in the Old Testament. Others do, indeed, waver in these commitments. The label "Progressive Dispensationalist" does not automatically identify a person's doctrinal stand on these crucial issues. And those who try to paint all individuals (or schools) with such a broad brush are guilty of misrepresenting the truth.

Moody Bible Institute requires all faculty members to agree

with, personally adhere to, and support the school's doctrinal distinctives, including those listed above. These are not negotiable. And neither Dr. Stowell nor I will ever waver in our commitment to these…and to all other…essentials of Biblical orthodoxy.

First of all, Dr. Dyer admits that there are professors at Moody who are teaching the new doctrine of Progressive Dispensationalism, which is something that has been previously denied by some of the leaders. The question now is how much of a deviation this doctrine is from Biblical orthodoxy, and how much harm it can do. Dyer maintains that, while some of the Progressive Dispensationalists (PDs) "waver in these commitments," the teachers at Moody do not. We are glad to hear this assertion, but there are other areas of Dispensational orthodoxy which are not covered by the above three doctrinal beliefs:

- **Literal Interpretation**. Moody has historically taught that the Bible is to be interpreted literally. However, as Dr. Walvoord, Dr. Lightner, Dr. Ryrie, Dr. Ice, Dr. Couch and many others have pointed out, the PDs' interpretation that Christ is *now* seated on the Throne of David is a serious departure from literal interpretation, and leads to spiritualization and allegorizing, which has always been deplored by orthodox dispensationalists.
- **Distinction in the programs for Israel and the Church.** It is one thing to say that Israel and the Church are two different peoples, but, as Dr. Lightner demonstrates (as we quoted in our article last month), it is quite another to understand that the Lord has *two different programs for Israel and the Church.* The PDs tend to blur the distinc-

tions between these two programs, and, if followed to their logical conclusion, this would lead to post-Tribulation Rapture, amillennialism, and Replacement Theology.

It is clear, then, that PD represents a deviation from some of the main doctrines of historic dispensationalism. The next question is how much harm the new doctrine may do. Dyer asserts that the PDs at Moody are supporting the three doctrinal imperatives he outlines, and, therefore, are welcome to continue as professors in the school. However, we believe that the new doctrine harms believers in Christ in several ways. Dr. Tommy Ice, in his review (published by the Pre-Trib Research Center) of a book co-authored by a professor at Moody, Dr. C. Marvin Pate, entitled *Doomsday Delusion: What's Wrong with Predictions About the End of the World?*, indicates that there is a movement away from the clear declaration of the promise of the Rapture:

> As has been typical of a number of these kinds of books in the last few years, their antidote to date-setting destroys a Believer's hope in an imminent Rapture and replaces it with the schizophrenic notion that Christ's Kingdom is "already/not yet." Even though Pate is a professor at Moody Bible Institute, *he is at odds with many of the beliefs that the school has historically been known for in the area of Bible prophecy.* This seems to be the trend in our day at most of the dispensational schools such as Dallas Seminary (our alma mater), Grace Seminary, Talbot, and others…. Unless we missed it, Pate and Haines do not even mention the Rapture, except when referring to it as a belief held by others. (Emphasis ours)

In addition, there is a movement away from the support of modern Israel as a harbinger of the Second Coming of Christ. Because of their blurring of the distinction between the programs the Lord has for Israel and the Church, there is now very little interest in what God is now doing in the regathering of Israel for the return of the Lord Jesus Christ, their promised Messiah. They see no correlation between Ezekiel's prophecy about the coming together of the Dry Bones and what is happening now, before our very eyes, in the new nation of Israel. Their attitude is that there may be a *future* for Israel in God's plan, but it has nothing to do with what is going on in the *present*. Thus, there is little teaching about the modern miracle of Israel and the preparation for the Tribulation, the Second Coming, and the glorious Millennial reign of Christ in the classrooms where Progressive Dispensationalism dominates or in the churches where their graduates preside. We praise the Lord for those schools, churches and individuals who continue to teach Blessed Hope of the Church and the truth of the regathering of Israel in these last days.

Along with Dr. McCall, I am concerned that a man of such reputation as Dr. Dyer is allowing himself to be put in a position of defending Progressive Dispensationalism. In the same publication, I gave my own response to Dr. Dyer below:

I'm disheartened to see this sort of letter from a distinguished theologian like Dr. Dyer. The question is why he defends a doctrine he doesn't believe himself. I am sorry that

"Dyer" Circumstances at Moody

Moody's President Stowell doesn't personally attempt to defend Progressive Dispensationalism, because it is obviously by his orders that this erroneous doctrine is taught at all. There certainly is a big difference between a full professor of theology who has always loved Israel and an erstwhile fundraiser like Stowell. Broader doctrines make for expanded enrollments and larger donations, and that, in addition to everyday anti-Israelism, is the major reason for this strange departure.

Perhaps we should ask Dr. Stowell, "Are you teaching that God is working through Israel *right now—today*?" and request that he give us the courtesy of a personal answer rather than ordering a busy professor to defend the indefensible.

Chapter 13
No Free Lunch at Moody ✦

by Thomas S. McCall, Th.D.

The detailed information given in the May *Levitt Letter* prompted some of our readers to write to key Trustees of Moody whose names and addresses were listed in the June issue. The responses received by the readers indicate that the Trustees are stating that the objections raised in our newsletter are not true. To support this, the Trustees are distributing a copy of Moody's recent doctrinal clarification document that was finalized and released to its undergraduate faculty in May 2000. This document is being mailed out in an effort both to discredit our claims of doctrinal drift, and also to reassure supporters of the school.

Maintaining the financial base is probably of utmost concern to the Trustees. There have been recent disclosures of un-

---

✦ In this September 2000 *Levitt Letter* article, Dr. McCall dealt with many details disclosed to us by friends at Moody Bible Institute who, like us, are alarmed with the shifting doctrines at that institution.

177

expected monetary shortfalls in Moody's annuities and trust arrangements, which led to the sudden dismissal of the school's chief financial officer earlier this year. This has resulted in austerity measures and belt-tightening in a number of areas in the undergraduate division, including faculty privileges in the undergraduate dining room. The Trustees are apparently using the doctrinal clarification document to quash unsettling rumors about changes in doctrine that might further threaten cash flow.

However, there are many questions about the doctrinal clarification document itself. We have known of its existence, are aware of its history and the process behind it, and are fully conversant with its content. The publication of this document, however, does not change the fact that, as reported in our May 2000 newsletter, there is a serious theological deterioration in the undergraduate division of Moody Bible Institute. Here are some of the questions that must be asked of the leaders of Moody.

First, why was there a need for a clarification document at all? Moody Bible Institute's 1928 Statement and the two policy statements on the modern tongues movement and feminism would appear to be all that was needed. The original statement emphasized the fundamentals of Christianity and made specific emphasis on premillennial/pretribulational eschatology. When the professors were interviewed for their positions, weren't these issues discussed with them prior to their being hired?

Second, why did it take four years, from 1996 to 2000, of committee work to clarify the five original articles and two policy statements?

Third, why did President Stowell and his chief administrators allow the faculty to remove "Here We Stand" (printed in 1986 with Stowell's imprimatur in it explaining where Moody stands) from the school's publications? Actually, we know why.

No Free Lunch at Moody

The faculty minutes show that one professor complained that he knew of at least half a dozen professors who would have to leave if "Here We Stand" was kept. Recently retired Dean of Education Dr. Howard Whaley then subsequently stated that the booklet was not official, and it was removed. Some now call the booklet "Here We Stood."

Fourth, why did Dean Whaley drastically reduce the initial 1999 clarification document from eight pages to eight short footnotes, a reduction in material of some 83%?! Again, we know why. When the faculty received its copy in March 1999 and discussed its content in faculty meetings, the minutes reflect such a strong, negative reaction to the material that another year was needed to rework it. Appeal was even made from within the faculty to stop the process completely. The initial document from the subcommittees was too specific, reflected material found in "Here We Stand," was incompatible with the new doctrine of Progressive Dispensationalism, and was thereby unacceptable to faculty members.

Fifth, why has Moody's administration allowed its faculty members to advocate egalitarianism/feminism in the classroom, in open forums, in written documents, and in the student newspaper, *Moody Student*? Our firsthand documentation since 1993 fully shows this to be a divisive problem. It violates the 1979 statement indicating that women should not have church pastoral roles.

Sixth, a study done by the Faculty Concerns Committee (1996-1997) reported to faculty a number of theological views in the faculty that troubled a "large number" of professors: anti-Messianic treatment of O.T. material, progressive dispensationalism, egalitarianism, charismatic issues, etc. Question: Why did the Academic Dean dismiss these reports and downplay them as non-policy items? A recent twist is the presence of professors who prefer to use the word "myth" to discuss O.T. material, especially early Genesis data. This confusion recently manifested itself in students in a senior colloquium. When asked what they thought about the creation material, they responded that they had been taught that it was myth: non-verifiable, non-historical, non-factual. Amazing!

Seventh, and finally, why has the administration allowed the faculty to change an important requirement for graduation? Prior to 1998, students had to "sign off" on the 1928 doctrinal statement. In 1998, faculty debated and moved to a blander "historic Christian faith," thereby eliminating some of Moody's unique dispensational elements as a requirement for seniors to graduate. In March 1999, Dean Whaley stated in a faculty meeting that there is coming a time when the Institute may have to graduate students who do not conform to the doctrinal statement. Why? What has changed?

Chapter 14
Progressive Dispensationalism: Its Deteriorating Effect

Throughout our battles with seminaries over the erroneous doctrine of Progressive Dispensationalism, many of those defending these institutions have stated that this new teaching is not a problem, it doesn't conflict with their doctrinal statements, it fits within acceptable parameters of understanding dispensationalism. We disagree. The correspondence we've exchanged with seminaries, the information sent to our office by staff and students alike, and, most importantly, Scripture itself, reveals that PD is a doctrine aimed at (whether purposefully or not) accommodating a wider theological base than what the doctrinal statements of these institutions require. Accommodation anytime in theology can potentially have a dangerous, deteriorating effect upon a school, its graduates, and eventually upon the Christian community as a whole.

History often repeats

Although Dallas Seminary, Moody, and others believe that

they can currently handle Progressive Dispensational perspectives within their faculty, it is quite probable that soon those perspectives and others will be handling the schools. Modern history is replete with examples of great institutions falling victim to "new teaching." Some of the top Ivy League universities began as Bible-teaching institutions. Fuller Seminary, from its inception, heralded biblical inerrancy, only to find itself embroiled in a battle for inerrancy in the '70s after certain faculty members began to degrade this essential doctrine. There are others…and there will be others, unfortunately.

A slippery slope

Dallas Theological Seminary, the historic bastion of dispensational belief and teaching, is known to have had some of the great teachers of dispensational doctrine as faculty and graduates, such as Walvoord, Pentecost, Ryrie, and others. However, these men are no longer as influential on campus as they once were. Despite the fact that their books are still used and that they still teach effectively in their retirement, many younger professors have been moving up the ranks of faculty and administration, men who are more willing to accommodate variant views on biblical beliefs, educational philosophies, vision of the school, etc. Every institution is entitled to and at times needs to adjust itself as the years pass in order to be most effective in its teaching. But, when those accommodations strike at the heart of their *core doctrines*, then the school is approaching the slippery slope.

Current indicators

One clear indication of this deteriorating effect at DTS is the fact that incoming and graduating students no longer need to sign the full doctrinal statement of the school, only the evangelical essentials. Thus, a student who is committed to covenant theology, which sees the Church replacing Israel, may attend, learn, and graduate still thoroughly covenantal in his beliefs—and that from the flagship institution of *dispensational* theology whose entire faculty must believe and teach dispensational doctrine! If this is true, then what need is there for the faculty to maintain its dispensational distinctiveness?

Progressive Dispensationalism is a teaching to watch carefully, because its influence will eventually undercut normative dispensational eschatology in the great institutions of our day. This, in turn, will filter down through students and then graduates and then to pastors and new seminary professors. This progressive cycle (no pun intended) can ultimately muddle the theological distinctiveness of dispensationalism and its common-sense approach to understanding the Bible and prophetic events, in particular.

Why Progressive Dispensationalism?

1. It broadens the doctrine of a given seminary so that more students will enroll. Since a majority of American students come out of churches which virtually never mention Israel or prophecy, the students will ultimately feel more comfortable with teaching that promotes the same errors. Once the seminaries get hooked on broadened doctrine as a key to increased enrollment, the doctrine will continue to take on more and more erroneous positions until the seminary is almost worthless as a Bible-teaching institution.

2. It avoids the complexities of End Times prophecies and spares its adherents from taking a position such as on the

Rapture or the obvious prominence of Israel in the world today.

3. It avoids the inconvenience of having to love the Jews, regard them as the Chosen People, or care about their homeland, Israel.

4. It allows for a corps of "young Turks," bright professors with a thirst for saying new and radical philosophies about Scripture. Their students, like the Greeks whom Paul confronted in Athens, hunger to "hear some new thing" (Acts 17:21).

5. It's the sort of doctrine that can be excused as being merely a new offshoot of an old and trusted Scriptural idea. But "Progressive Dispensationalism"—meaningless words— could well be called "Kingdom Now" or "Millennial Acceleration" or some other such name reflecting its error of placing a crucial Kingdom event in this age. By playing off the term "dispensation," the purveyors of the new doctrine hope to slip it in as a natural Scriptural idea and not simply an error.

It has become politically correct to avoid mention of or respect for Israel since the oil boycotts of the '70s and the Palestinian problems of the '80s and '90s. We still have a church of nothing but "our kind" and don't want to admit anyone too different from ourselves. Thus, doctrines which exclude Israel and the growing group of Jewish believers are more acceptable these days.

PD: Its Deteriorating Effect

Getting back to essentials

What are our needs today in these seminaries?

1. The need for current influential seminaries to get back to their roots and put doctrinal integrity over enrollment projections.
2. The need for new, sound institutions that do not waver on dispensational distinctives.
3. The need to equip pastors to teach their congregations more than "how-to" courses in coping with life today. The emphasis in training should be the life-changing Word of God, God's great plan for the ages, and our blessed hope. Get back to teaching Scripture!

Let's face it, the rapture is imminent, the time is short, the bulk of our lives will be lived after this life...the first thousand years of it in *Israel* where Christ will at that time ascend to the promised throne of David and reign over all the nations!

Chapter 15
The Trickle-Down Effect

As I review each of these three "battles" in which this ministry has been engaged for nearly ten years, I know some of you are thinking to yourselves, "What does it matter? This is nit-picking."

Well, the net effect of teaching anti-Israel doctrines is the production of anti-Israel graduates. While few graduating from Moody Bible Institute or Dallas Theological Seminary these days are very knowledgeable about Israel, some actually display hostility toward the Promised Land. One has to wonder if they'll hate the place during their whole 1,000 years there, or have they even been taught about the coming Millennial Kingdom?

This was, in fact, the experience of our staff theologian, Todd Baker, when he came across a fellow graduate of Dallas Theological Seminary who did not hide his animosity towards Israel on another Dallas radio program. As Todd recounts in the following article, this DTS graduate was interviewing a member of Louis Farrakhan's Nation of Islam, probably the most anti-Semitic and anti-Israel institution in the US.

Battles with Seminaries: Defending Israel

✡ ✡ ✡ ✡ ✡ ✡ ✡

"The Witness"

In May 1996, I was scanning the radio dial when I came across KPBC 770 AM, "The Witness." The host of the program was a graduate of Dallas Theological Seminary, and he was interviewing Thomas Mohammed, a Nation of Islam speaker. The host asked Mr. Mohammed about the Middle East situation, Israel in particular. Mohammed, a committed anti-Semite, replied with recycled, worn theories about the Jews controlling the world, Hollywood and the banking industries specifically. He claimed the Holocaust has been greatly exaggerated by the Jewish people and that Israel is the aggressor in the Middle East. He asserted that the Palestinians have been oppressed long enough, and the United States should stop supporting Israel and show their support for the Palestinians. He also said that Israel is holding many Palestinians in concentration camps, subjecting them to hideous torture.

Very few people called in to protest. In fact, there was almost no response from listeners. I didn't know if that was due to apathy on the part of Christians listening to the program or the radio station's low wattage resulting in a small audience (or perhaps the Christian public is growing as insensitive toward Israel and prophecy as Moody and Dallas Seminary graduates).

The host never even challenged Mr. Mohammed's hatred. He called him "brother," and seemed to take his statements at face value. I was so mortified, I called the radio show immediately, but the guest had already left. I explained to the host that everything Mr. Mohammed said was propagandist and laced with half-truths and outright lies, and that Islam is inherently anti-Semitic. To prove this, I quoted a sample passage from the

The Trickle-Down Effect

Koran to him, Sura 4, verses 40-50, in which it states:

> Among the Jews are those who displace the words of their scriptures, and say "We have heard, and we have not obeyed. Hear thou, but as one that heareth not; and look at us," perplexing with their tongues, and wounding the Faith by their revilings. But if they would say, "We have heard, and we obey; hear thou, and regard us;" it were better for them, and more right. But God hath cursed them for their unbelief. Few only of them are believers! O ye to whom the scriptures have been given! Believe in what we have sent down confirmatory of the scripture which is in your hands, ere we efface your features, and twist your head round backward, or curse you as we cursed the sabbath-breakers.

In one of Zola's books, *The Cairo Connection*, he supplies the Koranic thought, "Kill the Jew wherever you find him." I told the host the Jews are God's Chosen People unconditionally and eternally, and that a true Bible-believing Christian would support Israel and the Jews. God proved that He keeps His covenants when He regathered the Jews from all parts of the world, bringing them back to the Promised Land (persecution from Moslems notwithstanding).

The next day, the host gave me 15 on-air minutes (Mohammed got 60 minutes) to rebut. Off the air, I told him he needed to find someone who was expert in explaining Israel to others, someone like Zola Levitt. He asked me if I knew how to get in touch with this "Zola." I had never had any direct dealings with Zola's ministry, but I was well-acquainted with it, having watched Zola on television for years. I called Zola's son, Mark, the general manager of the ministry. He asked me to get a tape of the program or a transcript.

I immediately called the station and was told they would get that right out to me. What I got, instead, was a runaround for a full six weeks. When I finally did receive the tape, it had been edited down to 30 minutes. All of the most objectionable material had been deleted. Even so, there was sufficient evidence of what had been said for Zola to know how slanderous the remarks were against Israel and the Jews.

Zola went on the program. The host was very resistant to Zola. He asked, "If the Israelis bomb a bus, wouldn't you say that was wrong?" Zola replied, "When did they do that? The Israelis have never done that." The host couldn't respond to that. There was an undertone of antagonism in everything the host said to Zola, and he remained more accommodating to the Nation of Islam. He seemed outright anti-Semitic. He asked Zola, "What is a Jew?" Zola responded by telling him the Bible says a Jew is a physical descendent of Abraham, Isaac, and Jacob.

Zola explained that Israel is the one being persecuted in the Middle East, being taken advantage of in "peace talks," and that the Arabs' land holdings are 650 times the size of Israel. Israel is an important ally of the West, and we need to help them survive. "Christians should support Jews," Zola told the host, and "a person who doesn't isn't reading Scripture correctly."

The most shocking aspect of the interview with the Islamic "brother" is that it was aired on a supposedly Christian radio station. KPBC 770AM calls itself "The Witness." "What kind of witness?" I wondered. Certainly not a witness for God's Holy Land nor for His Chosen People, both of which should be supported by every Bible-believing Christian.

Chapter 16
How To Choose A Seminary

Dr. Thomas S. McCall, our Senior Theologian, has pro-
posed a four-question test in choosing a seminary or Bible
school. Assuming that you want Bible teaching and doctrines
that are accurate, then you must *first be assured that the seminary holds to the* **Deity of Christ***.* It is amazing that there are
Bible schools operating which do not consider our Lord to be
God incarnate, but they're all over the place. We call them liberal seminaries, and we gave an example in a recent newsletter
of a student of one of those who didn't care if Christ even ever
lived, according to what he said. Once the truth of the deity of
Christ is settled, other important matters such as His virgin birth,
substitutionary death and physical resurrection readily become
believable.

Secondly, you must insist on a seminary holding to the ***Inerrancy of the Bible.*** Obviously, if we're going to say that some
Scriptures are not accurate or literal, etc., in that way lies mad-
ness. Either the Bible is true or it's not true, and if we're going
to have a seminary at all, it must hold to the Bible containing no

error. There are some schools claiming to be conservative that are not willing to assert that the Scriptures are without error. They may use some slippery terms like, "the Bible *contains* the Word of God," or "the Bible is inerrant *in matters of faith*" (but not history). Beware these evasions.

Thirdly, the field of Eschatology is so critical today. Prophecy is more important than ever and, in particular, the Pre-Tribulation Rapture as we said above. When a school that was founded on the blessed hope of the imminent Pre-Trib Rapture begins to depart and waffle on the subject, it is a sign that both their eschatology (prophecy) and ecclesiology (knowledge of the church) are deteriorating.

*And finally, the **Truth** about Israel's importance is critical.* Does your seminary teach that God is moving in Israel today and that we are seeing prophecy fulfilled? Or does it teach, like the former Dallas Seminary professor, that Israel is merely a political entity and that "conceivably these people (the Jewish people) might be driven off the land" (his words on Christian radio!). Such is the fruit of doctrines like Progressive Dispensationalism. Many seminaries and Bible schools used to be friends of Israel and were convinced that the regathering of the Jewish people was a harbinger of the Second Coming of Christ. Recently, though, some leading evangelical schools are beginning to question "the promise of His coming" and the significance of modern Israel. Beware such statements as "prophecies about Israel won't be fulfilled until Christ's return." This is misleading and ignores all the preparation of Israel that must take place before and during the Tribulation.

So there you have Dr. McCall's four questions (like the four questions in Passover):

How to Choose a Seminary

- *D*eity of Christ
- *I*nerrancy of the Bible
- *E*schatology
- *T*ruth about Israel

Or

D.I.E.T. – a healthful and nutritious diet for believers!

Conclusion

For nearly a decade now this ministry has engaged in "battles" with seminaries over their professors, their textbooks, and their doctrines. As stated at the outset, our concern was not for those unbelieving and/or liberal-minded institutions that are devoid of true biblical integrity, but rather for the minority of conservative, evangelical seminaries and colleges that have traditionally been fortresses of doctrinal purity. We dare not give up on them, for from them emerge graduates who become the pastors, teachers, and leaders of the churches we attend. And if their "education" in these schools is increasingly watered down in the areas of biblical study which matter most, then the effects will soon filter down to our church members and Sunday school children.

This ministry, along with many others, has voiced its concerns and criticisms in ways that we feel will be most effective in urging correction within these institutions. At times, our efforts have been successful. Errant professors have left some schools, errant textbooks have been pulled from some classes, and a number of pastors-to-be have chosen other schools where doctrinal teaching can be trusted. Many hundreds of concerned

Battles with Seminaries: Defending Israel

Christians have called and written to these seminaries to find out the facts for themselves and, subsequently, to express their disapproval of aberrant teaching.

However, from those who should be the most alarmed with errors, the faculty, administration, and directors of these institutions, we have received the harshest responses, if they bothered to respond at all. Many wish to hide behind sterling public personas or simply wish not to enter the fray for fear of public backlash or exposure. Ignoring the problems or, worse, attacking the messenger, places these individuals and schools on dangerous ground.

Our belief is that many of these institutions sincerely feel that they can maintain doctrinal control because of their long-standing conservative reputations or because their "old guard" faculty will shield them from sliding down the slippery slope towards liberalism or compromise. This may indeed work for a short season, but as we pointed out in the preceding pages, new theologians have been rising in the ranks of the faculties and administrations of these schools to the point where now their voices are beginning to speak louder than the "old guard" theologians who actually built the schools' conservative reputations.

Once these tremendously popular schools like Moody, Dallas, Biola, Talbot, and others eventually fall off the deep end theologically (God forbid!), a majority of our new pastors, professors, and Christian leaders will be leading us and our children with watered-down or outright errant doctrinal views.

Many of our readers will know that this ministry is dedicated to Israel. I am a Jew and a Christian. Along with Paul, my desire is for my brethren, Israel, to be saved. We devote much of our efforts to bringing Jews to the Messiah. Concurrently, we also seek to teach Gentile believers the Scriptures, both Old

Conclusion

and New Testaments, with particular emphasis on God's care for and work in Israel, both now and in the future. Jewish believers are indeed a minority and, thus, the majority of our evangelical seminary and Bible college students are Gentile believers. Therefore, when we discover a trend in these institutions to minimize, de-emphasize, or alter God's teaching about the Jewish people and nation, we are alarmed. And what we've tried to accomplish here is to sound the alarm. As a result, a few have responded well, as this letter from Jane Roach of Bible Study Fellowships illustrates:

> Thank you for your concern for the accuracy of our lesson notes concerning Israel and Palestine. We have been making an effort to change them, but apparently, some have slipped through without our notice. May God bless your careful attention to detail!

I wonder if Moody Bible Institute, Dallas Theological Seminary, etc., ever considered correcting that sort of mistake rather than attacking competent messengers!

In closing, let me offer a few suggestions on how you can best prepare yourself for battle:

First, study to show yourself approved. Dig into the Scriptures, both Old and New Testaments. Read the Bible or listen to it on cassettes. Remember, this is God's inspired and inerrant Word to us. Hebrews tells us that it is "alive," and able to do spiritual surgery on our souls, so to speak. The late, great Bible expositor, Dr. Harry Ironside, who was a tremendously well-read minister, once commented near the end of his life that he wished he had spent more time reading just the Scriptures.

Second, read widely. There are many incredible books and teaching materials which you can trust from authors who are devoted to sound doctrine. This ministry, of course, carries many of them. Be like the Bereans in Acts 17:12 who constantly devoted themselves to studying what the apostles taught them in order to make sure it matched God's written Word. The better you know the Word of God itself, the better you will be able to distinguish between true and false doctrine in books, videos, television programs, and the like.

Third, our desire is that this book will call you to prayer. Pray for the leaders of these institutions, for their professors, for their boards of directors and administration officials. These individuals need God's wisdom and help to get them back on the right track. Don't forget to pray for your pastor and church leaders as well. Tell them that you're praying for them. It will encourage them greatly.

Finally, if you find errors in books, programs, and seminaries, take action. Write out what you think the problem is, then check it thoroughly with God's Word. Should you be one of those led to express your concerns, do it with prayerful confidence that God will not allow His Word to return without first accomplishing its purpose.

Doing battle is never easy and seldom rewarding, especially when struggling with fellow believers in the body of Christ. And yet, Scripture calls His people to a number of battle-related tasks, including defending the faith, exhortation, and even rebuking those who go astray. We must realize, however, that even in the household of faith, not everyone will agree nor will everyone respond graciously when confronted. Those who are led to call wandering sheep back to the fold, so to speak, are often attacked and wounded. It would be naïve for us to think otherwise. Remember, we are all finite and fallible humans, prone to sin, but forgiven and redeemed

Conclusion

by our loving Father through Jesus the Messiah. So when we present to you our "battles" with errant professors, schools, and doctrines, we trust you will use these events as occasions to hone and deepen your own faith in Christ, pray more fervently for Christians in influential positions, and express your concern when led of the Lord to do so.

May God bless you in your battle "for Zion's sake."

Epilogue:
Shaking Off the Dust *

by Zola Levitt

Scripture advises us to shake the dust off our feet when we have completed a mission, or at least done our all to complete it. Below is an update on our latest dealings with the seminaries, particularly Moody Bible Institute.

In the last few months, we have been distracted by the situation in Israel. That is our primary task, of course, and we consider it an honor to be called to the most important issue in Christianity today: the correction of the media distortions about Israel, and the reassurance that the place is in normal order for a democracy (and much safer than almost anywhere in the United States). The responsibility of attending to the Promised Land

---

* After this book was already in the hands of our editors, we finally received a more direct response from Dr. Stowell at Moody. We held the printing of this book until we felt our exchanges with the seminaries had concluded. This article originally appeared in our April 2000 *Levitt Letter.*

and the Chosen People is the most important job at this ministry.

Therefore we have been distracted from a secondary issue on the same subject, which concerns the seminaries: they ignore Israel and what is happening there at a time when God is obviously moving in that nation every day. Our best Bible schools have chosen, for seemingly very worldly reasons, to become like liberal seminaries and have quit teaching about Israel and prophecy in general. This is simply stupefying after nearly two thousand years of waiting for the restoration of the Chosen People to the Land, the rebuilding of the Temple, and the making of a peace covenant (evidently in the near future) with the personality who will become known as the Antichrist. Our Bible schools choose to turn away at precisely the time that all these things are taking shape.

And so it is our responsibility to step in and correct at least the most obvious of false doctrines being taught. The first one we have addressed is Progressive Dispensationalism. Dr. Tom McCall and I approached the seminaries over a period of time and pointed out the errors in this teaching. We even had a face-to-face meeting with Moody Bible Institute President Joseph Stowell in which we stressed the mistake in teaching. Stowell pretended that Moody did not have this problem. I know that many of you have written to Stowell and the others only to receive the usual reassuring seminary letters, off-point and patronizing. Please keep in mind that the seminaries don't belong to the Stowells or the Swindolls (Dallas Theological Seminary) or even to their board members. The seminaries belong to us—the Christian community. These *were* our finest schools.

This mixing up of the Kingdom and the Church Age, as with Progressive Dispensationalism, starts down a slippery slope that finally ends in Amillennialism and Replacement Theology. We have discussed those technicalities in previous issues. Suffice it to say here that we have shined a bright light on this false teaching of Progressive Dispensationalism. We should also mention that this is not the only false teaching going on. We will continue to offer constructive criticism—if necessary up to the time the Lord comes—to put a stop to all seminary prattling and worldliness.

In any case, here's a report on what has transpired in the last three months, especially at Moody Bible Institute. It seems that as a part of Moody's "kill the messenger" philosophy, a faculty and staff meeting was held in November, during which our ministry was thoroughly trashed. We are told Moody operates with a "gag order" where faculty is threatened with dismissal if they repeat what is spoken in their meetings (and we are aware of summary firings of faculty members with long and distinguished standing at that institution). Nevertheless, we received an anonymous letter from an attendee of that meeting who disclosed in full what was said. It's rather hard to put a gag on real believers; after all, the Lord stated, "Everyone that is of the truth hears My voice" (John 18:37).

As two of Moody's best-selling authors in the past, Dr. McCall and I took personal affront when we heard of the proceedings. First we verified the authenticity of the unsigned letter through two different sources at Moody. (A copy is available to you at this ministry. If you want to read it, please let us know.) After confirming the accuracy of the report, we contacted Moody at once. In particular, we addressed a certain professor who seemed to lead the charge against our ministry and who had been mentioned favorably in our newsletter previously.

The professor replied with a voluminous letter full of slippery denials, but we had corroboration that he did say the things the anonymous letter reported. Our next step was to send the anonymous letter to every member of Moody's board of directors, eighteen in all, asking that they look into the actions of the faculty and staff under the Stowell administration. We pointed out that the gag order intimidated those people too much for them to speak frankly to us and that we understood perfectly why the original letter was unsigned. We waited by the week for a reply.

That was a difficult moment because to our knowledge—and Dr. McCall and I have both taught at seminaries and attended similar meetings—we felt the board wasn't doing its job. A board of directors should take action when necessary to correct such major faults as this one. They are otherwise what our Lord called "blind guides." A seminary is not adequately supervised when it criticizes a sister ministry in a meeting attended by seventy faculty and staff members. Scripture teaches, "If you bring your gift to the altar and there remember that your brother has aught against you...be reconciled to your brother..." (Matt. 5:23-24). No member of Moody's faculty, administration or board has ever contacted us in any way except to brush us off for our troubles. We are not allowed to rock their boat. But of course, we're not the kind of people who willingly subscribe to the gag order mentality.

President Joseph Stowell finally wrote us a letter, which we guess was some sort of response to our letter to the board, but it contained nothing but more derision. If I quoted it, you'd be amazed at how the president of an evangelical seminary speaks to brothers in Christ who have come with an honest and godly purpose.

Finally, Dr. McCall took pen in hand, writing from the heart a letter which I signed with him. He pleaded with the board to respond to us and pointed out that this was their responsibility. Dr. Stowell had taken the position, like the presidents of The Criswell College and Dallas Seminary before him, that we were nothing but rabble-rousers and mischief-makers, and apparently persuaded the board that he could handle us. Dr. McCall's letter to the board is reproduced below.

Epilogue: Shaking Off the Dust

I would wrap up the situation as follows: The seminaries belong to the Christian public, not to the present administrations or board members. They are going liberal in the sense that they are teaching arcane doctrines, ignoring Israel and even the whole study of prophecy. Please see the letter by Andy in "Letters to Zola" of last month's issue for the fact that Dallas Seminary now offers only one prophecy course! A pastor friend of ours examined the Moody Bookstore recently and found utterly no books on prophecy!

We feel that it is the responsibility of the entire Christian public, not just this ministry, to protest, to complain, to withdraw funds, to keep students away or whatever it takes to get these seminaries back on a Biblical track. Otherwise, we'll lose them in the same way that we lost Harvard, Yale, Princeton, etc., which once were Bible-teaching academies. Past administrations of those celebrated institutions thought they were doing a great thing to turn them into large and well-endowed universities—Moody Bible Institute has established its own bank!—but they took them away from God in order to do that.

Our Lord taught that one cannot serve both God and money. The fault in every one of these cases is a love of money and all that it brings. We have pointed out before how broadening the doctrine of the seminaries will increase the enrollment of substandard students (likewise, an increase of their parents' donations, etc.), until in the end what we have is a big, rich, spiritually worthless and wholly ungodly institution.

We simply cannot allow these major seminaries to deteriorate in this fashion—and we include Talbot Seminary, Biola College and any number of other lesser institutions all sliding down the same slippery slope. Pray with us and take some action to correct the situation.

Battles with Seminaries: Defending Israel

Here is Dr. McCall's and my final letter to the board of Moody Bible Institute:

Dear Moody Board Member:

We received Dr. Stowell's letter of December 20, which we presume was intended to be a response to our letter of November 30 addressed to all the board members of Moody Bible Institute. We were very disappointed in the tone of his letter accusing us of having some kind of ulterior motive in our concerns about the doctrinal problems at Moody. As to the alleged slanderous remarks made about us personally and our ministry at a plenary staff and faculty meeting, the subject was cloaked in terms of confidentiality and summarily dismissed.

Rest assured that we (and many of our colleagues who are teaching the Word) are greatly disturbed over the doctrinal drift at Moody, Dallas, Talbot, Criswell and several other previously strong dispensational schools. All of them are moving down the slippery slope toward one or more errors such as Progressive Dispensationalism, Egalitarianism, mythologizing the Old Testament, removing the Christological content from the Messianic prophecies, promoting a negative attitude toward Israel, and adopting the potentially heretical concept of Process Theology. We are not saying all or even a majority of the teachers are adopting these views. However, a large number of teachers are advocating these aberrant positions, which are being tolerated by the administration as well as the board. It appears that these teachers are gaining more and more control over the curricula, particularly the theological emphasis at Moody and the other schools.

This information is not hidden in theological circles, but is widely known and discussed with much concern. Books and articles have been written on the subject. The general Christian public, however, is only vaguely aware that there are some serious shifts in doctrine going on in these institutions, but have a difficult time identifying the rather complex problems. They do realize that many of the current graduates teach the Gospel and the Scriptures in a considerably different manner than the previous graduates. In the meantime, the administrations of the various schools proclaim publicly that there is no change, saying that the doctrinal position remains the same. All the while, in a growing number of classrooms, the students are being taught something very different. If someone attempts to alert the schools on behalf of the supporting evangelical public, the administrations tend to attack the messengers rather than addressing the truly serious cancerous problems plaguing the schools.

If all of this is true, what is to be done? Who can correct the problems? Who is responsible? The founders assumed that a strong doctrinal statement and a spiritually astute board of directors would make sure that the schools would remain theologically sound. Ultimately, the supporting public looks to the board of directors to assure that the schools remain sound Scripturally and financially. This is not an easy task, and it involves the difficult work of investigation and evaluation. Nevertheless, the board cannot abdicate its responsibility to reassure the supporting Christian public.

Please advise us at the earliest just what steps the board of directors at Moody will take to investigate and evaluate the doctrinal problems mentioned above, as well as the alleged slanderous remarks that may have been uttered against us and our ministry. Our readers and television viewers would be greatly encouraged if we could report to them that the board is coming to grips with the problems mentioned herein in order to make any corrections that are warranted. Please know that our next publication date will be in about three weeks.

We look forward to hearing from you soon.

The only reply was a letter from board president Paul H. Johnson enclosing Moody's doctrinal statement and telling us that the faculty signed it with integrity, which, as we pointed out, could not be true. None of the eighteen board members discussed our complaint or owned up to the faculty meeting and what was said.

One final postscript to our battles with these seminaries. Just before going to print, our office received two email letters, one from a concerned listener of a Moody radio program, and the other from a pastor who recently graduated from Dallas Theological Seminary. We share with you excerpts of their experiences:

I was listening to Moody's Mid-Day Connection show and they were interviewing an author by the name of George Grant who wrote a book called *The Micah Mandate*. As I was listening to the author take calls, a caller…said "that because the church is now Israel, it is important for the church (i.e. Israel) to rise up against evil in our culture and bring justice as Micah did." The author agreed. I contacted the radio show…[and said that] I had a real concern about the statements that were being made about the church replacing Israel. She said, "If we can fit you in, we'll call you back."

Conveniently, they did not call me back. As I continued to listen to the program, absolutely NO ONE challenged this issue and it was scary how many people called in with this same idea, which was the springboard of the author's book. It's discouraging that so many people are in the dark where Israel is concerned and if they'd just read Romans chapter 11, it's very clear that the church has NOT replaced Israel.

After our experience, it is no wonder errors like these are being propounded more frequently from Moody Bible Institute and their affiliate ministries.

Now, the letter from this disappointed pastor:

I have recently been reading your letters in regards to PD and the atmosphere at DTS. In one of the letters from last year, you make reference to the sad fact that recent DTS students neither know or care about Israel and related theological matters about Israel. I am a recent DTS grad (MABS 2000). I wish you to know that I am a strong supporter of you and the traditional view of Israel. Also, as one who has recently been "inside" the school, I can tell you that there is a strong emphasis on PD by the theological faculty…to the extent that I feel my Eschatology course was a waste of my time and money. It was taught entirely from a PD emphasis. The main text was the Bock and Blaising book. None of the major texts by Walvoord or Pentecost were required. The sad thing is that I went to DTS with the main idea that I would have a solid grounding in

Eschatology.

Despite our attempts to sound the alarm over the years that theological drifts in core beliefs at our best schools would filter down through succeeding generations of graduates and thus church leaders, the pastor above poignantly confirms what we've been saying for ten years. The tragedy is that many of his fellow graduates probably didn't even notice a problem!

Throughout this long struggle for doctrinal purity in our Bible schools and seminaries, our greatest concern has been that an increasing number of schools, publications, and programs have begun to de-emphasize the importance of Israel as a nation and as the major player in End Times prophetic fulfillment. Of course, we expect such attitudes from the non-Christian community, fueled by the slanted reports of CNN and other major news outlets. We don't expect this same dangerous perception to creep into our "boot camps" for Christian workers, especially in those which have traditionally been supportive of Israel and her right to the land. To deny or denigrate God's working among His Chosen People now and in the future, as Scripture clearly reveals, is to allow compromise to subtly sneak into one's core beliefs. What will Moody or Dallas or Criswell and other schools look like doctrinally in five or ten years? Will they completely turn their backs on key doctrines and rich biblical traditions? Only God knows how far each one will slip down this dangerous slope, but we, you and I both, are responsible to

Epilogue: Shaking Off the Dust

sound the alarm and even enter the fray in order to bring these institutions back to Scriptural purity and right thinking.

May God bless you as you do!

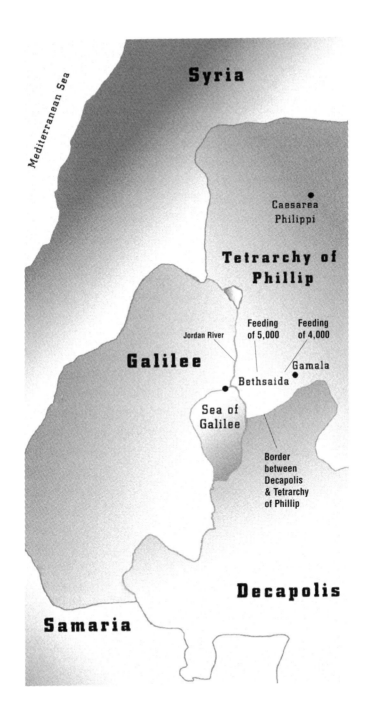

Recommended Resources

<u>From Zola Levitt Ministries</u>:

Anti-Israel Tapes (AS@)

Broken Branches—Replacement Theology (BBRT)

Israel's Right to the Land (IRL)

Israel By Divine Right (IDR)

Once Through the New Testament (ONT)

Also, ask about enrolling in our 12-part course: *The Institute of Jewish-Christian Studies*

✡ ✡ ✡ ✡ ✡ ✡ ✡

To order these resources or for further information about our other resources, please contact us for a free catalog:

Toll-Free order line: 1-800-WONDERS

Write: Zola, Box 12268, Dallas, Texas 75225

Email: staff@levitt.com

Internet: www.levitt.com

Don't forget to check out our online bookstore!